Frank Stockton Dobbins

The Ansons in Asiatic Temples

Frank Stockton Dobbins

The Ansons in Asiatic Temples

ISBN/EAN: 9783744757560

Printed in Europe, USA, Canada, Australia, Japan

Cover: Foto ©ninafisch / pixelio.de

More available books at **www.hansebooks.com**

THE ANSONS

IN

ASIATIC TEMPLES.

BY
REV. FRANK S. DOBBINS.

PHILADELPHIA:
AMERICAN BAPTIST PUBLICATION SOCIETY,
1420 Chestnut Street.

CONTENTS.

CHAPTER I.
SETTING OUT ON THE JOURNEY.................. 7

CHAPTER II.
A TRICYCLE TRIP TO ASAKUSA, TOKIO.......... 23

CHAPTER III.
AN AFTERNOON IN SHIBA, TOKIO............... 38

CHAPTER IV.
A JIN-RIKI-SHA JAUNT TO DAI BUTZ............ 54

CHAPTER V.
OVER THE MOUNTAINS TO KIOTO............... 71

CHAPTER VI.
THE SACRED CITY OF KIOTO.................... 86

CHAPTER VII.
TO THE LAND OF TEAS AND QUEUES. 102

CHAPTER VIII.
FROM SHANGHAI TO PEKIN.................... 118

CHAPTER IX.
THE STORY OF "CHINESE GORDON.".............. 137

CHAPTER X.
HOUSEKEEPING IN CANTON.................... 152

CHAPTER XI.
IN THE LAND OF THE WHITE ELEPHANT......... 171

CHAPTER XII.
UNDER THE SHADOW OF SHWAY DAGON........ 187

CHAPTER XIII.
FROM RANGOON TO MADRAS.................... 205

CHAPTER XIV.
Juggernaut and Kali 221

CHAPTER XV.
Overland Through India 242

CHAPTER XVI.
In Moslem Lands 260

CHAPTER XVII.
The Invalid's Journey Home 274

THE ANSONS IN ASIATIC TEMPLES.

CHAPTER I.

SETTING OUT ON THE JOURNEY.

THE Hoyt Mission Band had just closed its meeting. As the little folks stood about, putting on their coats and hats, it was very evident that something had greatly excited them. There was an unusual bustle and stir, as the tongues were wagging in a much livelier manner than during the meeting just closed; and there was good reason for it, as we shall see.

Bertie and Bessie Anson had been living in Alton for six years past. Their father was the Pastor of the First Church. Just before coming to Alton he had been greatly moved by the speech of a returned missionary, and had determined to give himself to the work of winning the Chinese to Christ. But his physician told him that he was not strong enough to stand a life-long residence in that country, and he was forced to give up his cherished purpose.

When he settled in Alton, he determined to become better acquainted with the work of foreign missions, and to try to awaken in his people an interest in them. So he set for himself a course of study on the geography and history of Asia, and began to read of the manners of the strange peoples occupying that continent. He found this an excellent diversion from his ordinary studies. Of course, his little boy and girl, then eight and six years old, became interested also in their papa's books and maps and pictures.

The people did not care much for missions, as Mr. Anson soon learned; but the reason of this was, that they knew scarcely anything about them. The first thing he did was to buy a

SETTING OUT ON THE JOURNEY. 9

Magic Lantern and a number of slides, and with the aid of these he gave a series of Friday evening lectures. Of course, the people came to see the pictures, and soon began to care more for the salvation of the idolaters. After a little while the young folks planned to organize a Mission Band, and to take up in earnest the study of missions. Mr. Anson presided at their meetings, and gave the little folks the benefit of his own learning. The Band had made such progress, that in four or five years they had made imaginary journeys in almost every country of Asia. They had held festivals, given entertainments, and prepared "Japanese tea-parties," all in addition to the gift of quite a sum of their own money to the missionary workers in Swatow.

Mr. Anson had a pet project; for this he had been carefully saving his money during the six years past. It looked as if he would have to wait a great many more years before he would be able to carry out his plan, when he received news of the death of a relative, to whom he had once rendered important services, who had left him nearly five thousand dollars. At once his mind was made up that he should take his family and make the long wished for tour of the temples and missions of the East. In this way, he felt that he could become well acquainted with the missionaries and their fields of labor; and so, perhaps, be of as much service to the Master in stirring up the hearts of Christians at home, as if he had gone to China as a missionary.

This it was that had caused such a stir among the members of the Hoyt Mission Band, for Bertie and Bessie had just told them of the intended journey.

"Oh, how I wish that I was going!" "Won't you write us long letters and tell us all that you see?" "When will you go?" "They won't eat you up, will they, out there?"

How the questions poured out! It seemed wonderful that it was to be a real journey; that with their own eyes Bertie and Bessie were to see the temples and the mission chapels of which they had read in *Little Helpers* and *The Helping Hand;* that they were to go about among the queer folks of whom the missionaries had written.

The days of preparation quickly passed by, and the Anson family were ready to start on their journey around the world. Mr. Anson had determined to burden himself with just as little baggage as possible. So we see the family party, on a bright Monday morning, seated in the Pullman car, dressed in rough and tumble suits, and ready to enjoy, to the full, their journey from the very beginning. To Bertie and Bessie it was a new experience to travel for more than a few hours. "It was just like a picnic," Bessie said, as the porter brought them their great lunch basket. When night came, their seats were drawn together, mattresses and sheets and blankets spread over them, and a bed pulled down from the ceiling of the car, and curtains hung before them. Then Bertie and his papa climbed up into the upper berth, while Bessie and her mamma slept in the lower one. It was a long while before the children could get to sleep; they were so excited with the leaving home, and were so often disturbed as trains rushed past them. It was a night and an experience that they never forgot.

The party stopped for a day in Chicago, to get rested and to prepare for the journey across the prairies and mountains to San Francisco, where they were to take the steamer for Japan. At Ogden they stopped again, to go up to Salt Lake, and to see the great Mormon city. After a ride of a little more than six days and nights in the cars, they reached San Francisco. Here Bessie took the chance of writing to one of her friends who occupied the same seat with her in school, and who was the Secretary of the Hoyt Mission Band:

SETTING OUT ON THE JOURNEY. 13

"Occidental Hotel, San Francisco.

"My Dear Nellie: Oh, how I wish that you and all the girls could be with me! It all seems so funny. We are awfully tired of riding in the cars. I would like to tell you about the Indians we saw, and their babies, 'pappooses,' as they call them; they were awfully dirty, I thought, and their papas and mammas were not any cleaner. When somebody said, 'There's an Indian,' oh, how it made my heart jump! But I don't feel half so afraid now. And then the Chinamen; we saw more and more of them the nearer we came to California. They look so clean (papa says it is only on the outside), and they go about so quietly.. But, how funny their talk seems. 'Supposee, missie, you wanchee one cup tea, me catchee.' 'You, Melican girlee?' 'Me sabee.' They call this 'pidgeon English,' or business English.

"We climbed up, up, up the mountains from Nebraska, then we went down the Rockies, and then right up and over the Sierra Nevadas. At one place they took us on board a great ferry-boat, locomotive, cars, and all. The cars do not come right into San Francisco, but they run into Oakland and out on a great wharf several miles long; then the people get into two-storied ferry-boats, and are taken over the bay into the city. Bertie says that a man told him that there are three railroads across the continent now, one up north, through Dakota to Oregon, one down south, through New Mexico and Southern California, and the one we came on, through Nebraska, Wyoming, Nevada, and so to San Francisco.

"On Tuesday, a girl named Rubie Larrison came to see us with her papa, who is a deacon in the church here. I like her very much, and I am going to see her some day at her home. Last Sunday, we went to church in Oakland, and I sat with Rubie. In the evening, we went to the Chinese Mission School; it was a queer Sunday-school. Every class had just one pupil and one teacher. The Chinamen all dress just as they do

SETTING OUT ON THE JOURNEY. 15

in China, with their 'pig-tails,' and all. They sing in Chinese mostly. I had all I could do to keep from laughing at them. Papa is going to take one of the Chinese 'boys' with him on the steamer; his name is Ah Ching. He has been very sick, and the missionary teacher wants to keep him out of the steerage. By going with papa he can be in the cabin most of the time.

"The folks that we have met tease us about being sea-sick, and they ask us to try all sorts of things to keep off sea-sickness. Papa went to the doctor's yesterday, and he gave him some powders in a tin box. We all have to take them; they taste just like salt. They are marked Bromide of Sodium; but I don't know what that is.

"Well, I must not write any more, because it is bedtime. Please give my love to all the girls.
"Your friend,
BESSIE ANSON."

It took some time to make all the arrangements for the sea voyage. State-rooms had to be secured, money had to be exchanged, tickets bought, and every so many other little things to be attended to. Under the guidance of Rubie Larrison and her papa, the children went to Woodward's Gardens and to the Cliff House, to see the seals come up out of the sea and climb up the rocks. At another time they went to the smelting works, and saw them refining gold and silver; and then, to the Mint, where it was turned into coin. On another day, guided by a policeman, they went through "China-town," among the opium dens, and into the "joss-houses," where the children saw for the first time the idols of the heathen. It seemed a strange thing to find so many heathen temples in Christian America. In one of these temples, three idols sat side by side; they represented Buddha past, present, and to come; and all parts of the temple, as well as the idols, were decorated with color and gilding. While the children were in the "Joss-house of the Three Precious Buddhas," a poor woman came in, and, kneeling with her head to the floor, began to mumble over her prayers. It brought the tears to Bessie's eyes, and filled the hearts of all with sadness, that she should be praying to the wooden idols that could not hear, while a loving, living Saviour stood waiting to help her.

Mr. Anson found out that quite a number of missionaries were to sail on the same steamer with his own party; and, as he had some letters of introduction to officials of the Steamship Company, he managed to have it arranged that his party and the missionaries should have rooms close together, and that they should eat at the same tables. He was also able to get into the good graces of the captain, through the influence of these friends, and so received many little kindnesses during the voyage. Among the missionaries were a gentleman and his wife, who had lived twenty-five years in China, and another and his wife, who had lived a short time in Japan, and who were going back again with their little son, a child of three years old.

The rest were all new to the work; they were a medical missionary and his wife, and four young ladies and two young gentlemen. This made a very pleasant company; and Mr. Anson was delighted that he had such a chance of becoming well acquainted with the missionaries.

Finally the day came for starting on the long voyage of three or four weeks across the Pacific Ocean. The steamer's decks were crowded with friends, who had come aboard to say a last good-bye. Here and there might be seen a lady passenger, looking with envious eyes upon those who were so fortunate as to have friends to bid them a farewell. Then the bell rang the hour, a Chinese cabin-boy beat the gong, and the officers called out: "All aboard and all ashore." The great ropes were drawn in, the gangway drawn up, the tug was made fast to the steamer, the pilot took his place, the command was given, and the great vessel was towed out into the bay. Then the tug's ropes were cast off, the whistles blew a farewell, the engineer's bell was rung,.

the great screw began to turn, and, by its own power, the steamer moved grandly down the bay. As they passed, the whistles of the smelting-works blew a farewell to the missionary party, who had visited them a few days previous.

As everything had been arranged in the staterooms the Anson party were to occupy, they remained upon deck, determined to see the last of the land. Very little motion was felt, and our friends were congratulating themselves upon their comfortable feelings. Just as the vessel passed through the Golden Gate, out upon the Pacific Ocean, the motion of the swell began to be felt, and when well across the bar, the rolling and pitching began. One after another went below to find a place to lie down. Bessie was quite amused as little Charlie wanted to know what made the water jump up to the clouds and then away down again, and what made him feel so funny. By-and-by, the "Oh mys" were heard, as one or another suffered the distresses of sea-sickness. The Anson family kept up very well, thanks to the medicine which they had taken by the doctor's direction, though it did not entirely prevent the sickness.

Bertie soon made friends with the officers and passengers, and, boy like, asked any number of questions. He pried into everything. For awhile he stood watching the wheelman, after the pilot had gone ashore; then he looked into the coops where the sheep, and the ducks, chickens, turkeys, and pigeons were kept; then through the hatchways he watched the working of the engines.

After awhile, the purser came on deck and began to talk with him. After a little banter about his not being sick, the purser began to talk of the passengers. Bertie had always looked upon missionaries as a sort of heroes, and was much taken aback when the purser ventured to sneer at them and their work.

As the days passed by and he became better

acquainted with the purser and with some of the passengers, more doubts were put into his mind, and he, himself, began to doubt if the missionary work was really of any use, and to wonder if it was not all folly, after all. He could not tell these thoughts to his father, he felt, and so he determined that he would carefully watch the missionaries and listen to their talk, and so see if they were in earnest; and that when he went through Japan and China he would see for himself as to the real state of the heathen, and just what good or evil the missionaries might be doing. He might have told his father all about his doubts; but, with the conceit so common to boyhood, he preferred to see for himself and to reason the thing out alone.

Every morning and evening, the missionaries and the Anson family gathered together in a corner of the dining-room for "family prayers." On Sundays, they gained the great privilege of having service in the "Social Hall." Often they would cluster about the piano and sing some of the grand old gospel hymns; and on warm, pleasant nights would draw their chairs together upon the deck and send the sweet sounds out upon the air. They seemed greatly to enjoy each other's company; though they belonged to different denominations, they were one in their trust in Christ, and one in wishing to give his gospel to the heathen. So day after day passed, varied by storms and calms, yet one day very much like every other. On the twentieth day of the voyage, the captain assured the passengers that they should see land on the morrow, and, with this joyous expectation, they "turned in" early.

CHAPTER II.

A TRICYCLE TRIP TO ASAKUSA, TOKIO.

BRIGHT and early the next morning, Bertie rose and went on deck, half expecting to see land close at hand. Nothing was to be seen, however, but the same great circle where sea and sky seemed to come together. Just then the quartermaster came to the captain's cabin, and called out:

"Land ahead, sir."

"Where?" said Bertie.

"Right off there. Can't you make it out, sir?"

Bertie looked and looked in vain. Finally, he went to his state-room and brought his glasses, but even then he could not see it. Just then the captain came from his room.

"Where is the land, captain? I can't see it."

The captain scanned the horizon before them.

"Why, right there. Just keep looking at that point, a little above the horizon; you can only tell it from the waves, because they move, while it is steady. You will soon see more of it."

After breakfast, when they came on deck again, they could see, quite plainly, a point stretching up into the sky.

"It is Fuji-yama, the great mountain of Japan," said one of the missionaries who had been over to Japan before.

As the forenoon passed away, birds came flying about the vessel—not the gulls which had always been flying about the stern of the steamer all the voyage across the ocean—but land birds. The saw-like line of the horizon became more distinct, as they came nearer to the mouth of the bay of Yedo; they passed many Japanese fishing junks with their square sails; and off to the south they could see a long trail of smoke left by a steamer, which had disappeared below the horizon.

For several days the crew had been busy

polishing up the brasses, and scouring and scrubbing generally; now every rope was coiled up nicely, the covers were taken from the furniture, the carpet's covering removed, and the whole vessel was put in holiday trim.

While yet some distance down the bay, the steamer was sighted, and a signal gun was fired from an American man-of-war, which announced to the people of Yokohama the arrival of the American mail steamer. Soon the bay was all alive with little boats, sculled by almost naked boatmen; and little steam launches were seen rushing towards the steamer as she came up to her buoy and was made fast. The gangway was lowered, and people began to go and come.

Among the first to come aboard were some missionaries from Yokohama, who sought those who were to join their mission in Japan. These all went off together. Shortly after, the Anson family took their places in a hotel launch, and were very quickly in their rooms, overlooking the bay, where they could see the steamer riding at her buoy nearly a mile from shore.

Bertie and Bessie were impatient to go out into the native town; but as in the excitement of getting to land they had eaten no "tiffin"— as they call the noonday luncheon in the East— they were compelled to wait a little while. While they were at tiffin, a Japanese servant brought in a card to Mr. Anson, saying:

"Gentleman, he want see you."

Mr. Anson found it to be an old college friend, who had been in Japan for about six years past, and who had seen his name in the list of passengers just arrived. At once he asked Mr. Anson to his home; but Mr. Anson feared that this might put his friend to considerable trouble, as his "bungalow" was small, so he declined; but gladly accepted the offer of guidance.

When the family were all together, they began to talk over their plans with Mr. Benton. He advised them to spend two or three days sightseeing in Tokio, the capital, then to proceed overland to Kioto, turning aside on the way to see the gigantic idol, Dai Butz; from Kioto they could proceed to Kobé, where they would take steamer for Shanghai, China. After considerable discussion, they decided on adopting this route. For this afternoon they concluded to stay within the foreign settlement, to go to the book stores and get a map of Japan, a guide book, and some other supplies. They found that the houses and stores of the foreigners were built mostly of stone and tiles, with tile roofs; that there were no sidewalks, and that people of almost all nationalities were to be seen going to and fro. In their rambles they passed by several large stone buildings, from whose windows came a delightful fragrance. Into one of these Mr. Benton took them, and they saw several hundred women standing before charcoal fires in stone braziers, kneading some sort of leaves. This they found to be the tea-leaves, and they were being "re-fired" before packing them in boxes to send to America.

At an early hour the next morning, the party were at the railroad station, accompanied by Mr. Benton, who was to be their guide in Tokio. After a ride of eighteen miles, they reached the capital. Here a friend of Mr. Benton's met them at the station. They were soon seated in their *jin-riki-shas*, a carriage holding one or two persons, and pulled by two Japanese coolies. Mr. Benton's friend, Mr. Granger, had brought his tricycle, which had seats for two, and he invited Bertie to sit beside him, so that he might explain to him the persons and places that they passed.

So they trundled along up the Ginza Avenue, by the side of the street cars, under the wires from which the electric lights were suspended, and by houses that were half foreign looking. It seemed to Bertie and Bessie that they had need of a half-dozen pairs of eyes apiece to see all the curious objects that they passed. Up one street and down another, it seemed a perfect maze, and yet the sun steadily shone upon their backs, so that they knew they were not going around and around.

"Where are you taking us to?" Bertie asked Mr. Granger.

"To the great Temple of Asakusa, the temple that is more crowded with worshipers than any other temple in the city."

"Why do you go to the temple? Are there not other things more worth seeing?" Bertie asked.

"No," said Mr. Granger; "the temples of Asakusa and of Shiba, where we are going this afternoon, are the most famous sights of Tokio. While we are up in this part of the city we may run over to Uyéno Park and see the Government Museum; but you will soon see that the temples are far more curious and interesting."

"Of course," said Bertie, "I have heard of temples; but I really do not know just what they are. What kind of a place is this temple of—what do you call it?"

"A temple is not like a Protestant church in America, but rather like the Roman Catholic cathedrals and shrines. You know that Buddhism—to which these temples belong—and Roman Catholicism are, in some respects, as much alike as two peas in the same pod. Within the temple grounds, as you will see, there is quite a collection of buildings—the temple proper, the priests' houses, a preaching hall, and the like; but you will soon see for yourself."

Mr. Granger and Bertie were in the lead, and the *jin-riki-shas* came after them. The roads were so hard and smooth, and the tricycle so light and easily propelled, that they had to wait quite frequently for the pullers of the *jin-riki-shas* to catch up. Sometimes they would turn aside from the direct road, in order to see some of the wayside shrines or idols, or to glance into some of the houses or stores, whose fronts were entirely open to the street.

After a little they came to a place where great

numbers of *jin-riki-shas* were standing, and Mr. Granger said:

"Here we must get down."

So, leaving their tricycle and their wraps in the care of the *jin-riki-sha* men who had brought the rest of the party, they turned up a narrow street, made only for pedestrians. The lane was lined with booths on either side, where candies, sugared beans, and various toys were the chief things sold. Three or four hundred yards further, they came to a gigantic gateway, guarded by two hideous wooden idols, a sort of Gog and Magog. On the wooden gratings before these idols were hanging huge straw sandals, locks of hair, pictures, and other votive offerings.

A little before the gate, they turned to the right, and passing by some tea-houses, where pilgrims were quietly sipping tea, they went to the Revolving Library. In a room about twenty feet high, Bertie and Bessie saw a bookcase attached to the ceiling and the floor in such a way that it could be turned around.

It contains the Buddhist Bible, of over three thousand volumes.

'As nobody could ever read it through," said the priest in attendance, to Mr. Granger; "not even in a life-time, Shaka will accept it as read through once, if a man will make the case revolve three times."

Bertie and Bessie could not budge the case, but Mr. Anson was able to do so, without much effort.

Passing by a five-storied pagoda, they came to the temple proper. Climbing up some steep steps, they entered the vestibule, where the crowd were worshiping. Immense lanterns were hung from the ceiling, in and among which darted the sacred pigeons. An old woman sat by an incense-burner, and for a small coin threw a pinch of incense upon the charcoal fire within. In front of the main altar was a great coffer, into which the devotees threw a coin before beginning to pray. Then they would rub the palms of their hands together, and tell their beads, as they mumbled their prayers, looking up to the idol within. As fast as one would go another would take his place. Some would clap their hands aloud, to attract the attention of the goddess within to the prayers they were about to offer. Occasionally one would go to a priest, buy a written prayer, put the paper in his mouth and chew it into a "spit-ball" and then throw it at the wire grating before the idol; if it stuck fast, his face would brighten up with the feeling that the prayer would be heard; but if it fell, then he would go away looking down-hearted. Once in awhile a well-dressed man or woman would pass through a side door giving a fee to the priestly door-keeper, and proceed to worship in the seclusion within the grating, away from the crowd.

Just here Bessie noticed some mothers approaching, carrying their little babes, and they were sickly, delicate, wizen-faced little things; the babes were carried on the mother's back, between their inner and outer garments.

"What are *they* going to do?" asked Bessie.

"Watch them, and you will see," said Miss Kirby, a missionary who had joined the party.

The mothers drew near to an ugly little wooden idol, placed on a small pedestal, and then reaching over their shoulders, took the hand of the little baby, and first rubbed it on the old idol's face, and then on the sick or sore spot on her child. The idol's nose, eyes, and ears were almost rubbed off. "That is Bindzuru-sama, the God of Healing," said Miss Kirby, "and the mothers think that he will help their babies to get well. If they get better, then the mothers bring their bibs and fasten them about the idol's neck, as you see them."

Just here, an old priest came from a stand on one side of the altar, and holding up a gilded shrine by the ring in its top, asked Miss Kirby, in Japanese, of course, if the little girl did not want to buy a shrine of Kwanon-sama, the Queen of Heaven and Goddess of Mercy.

"What for?" said Miss Kirby.

"Why, to take home with her, and to say her prayers to, that Kwanon may protect her."

"Kwanon can't protect her," said Miss Kirby;

SHRINE OF KWANON.

"that is only a piece of wood; you ought to look to the true God, in heaven, for protection."

On the invitation of another priest, the party, first taking off their shoes, went in through the side door, around the inner shrine. At one side was a private altar, where private "masses" were said. Here a priest was building a little bonfire of splints, on a low altar, and throwing into the fire, every now and then, a pinch of incense. What, with the ringing of a small bell, the tapping the incense boxes with his "bauble," the telling of his beads, and the mumbling of a sentence of Sanskrit over and over again, it seemed to the children a singularly senseless jargon. Miss Kirby had often seen it before, but Bessie noticed, as she stole a glance into Miss Kirby's face, that tears of pity were falling from her eyes.

On the main altar rested a shrine of the goddess of the temple, and in and around were great numbers of smaller idols. On one side was a gigantic mirror, presented to the temple by a wrestler, as a votive offering. In the temple grounds without, were all sorts of exhibitions: a wax-works' show, monkeys, tamed birds, performing dogs, photographers' galleries, and dear knows what all.

By this time our friends were thoroughly tired and heart-sick. They quickly found their *jin-riki-shas* again, and Mr. Granger and Bertie their tricycle, and they were soon whirling away towards Shiba; where, after luncheon they were to spend the afternoon.

CHAPTER III.

AN AFTERNOON IN SHIBA, TOKIO.

AFTER leaving Asakusa, our friends went first to the public park at Uyéno, where there is a very large and very ugly idol of Buddha, made of bronze, a weak and feeble imitation of the great idol at Kamakura. After rambling about the park, visiting the great museum, and looking into some of the temples scattered through the grounds, a search for luncheon began. It was too much out of the way to go to Tsukiji, where most of the foreigners live, so they rode down the *Tori*—as the chief street is called—and finally drew up before a fine large building, along whose front was strung a row of lanterns. Passing through the kitchen, which, in Japanese restaurants, is almost always in the front of the house, after removing their shoes, they climbed up a broad ladder to a pretty room above. By sliding screens, the host shut off this room from all the others. The floor was covered by mats made of straw, each six feet long and three feet wide, and about two inches thick. There was no furniture in the room.

The Americans seated themselves upon the floor, sitting on their heels just like the Japanese; this seemed easy enough for a little while, but soon their limbs became stiff and aching, and they were glad to push them out behind them. Two or three chubby-faced, red-lipped girls slipped softly through the sliding screens, and, bowing to the floor, began to express their sense of the honor conferred upon the house by their visitors. They had brought with them a fire-box, with a handful of lighted charcoal, and a tray with tobacco and tiny pipes upon it. This last Mr. Granger sent right away, to the astonishment of the waiter girls.

"This is jolly," said Bertie.

"Yes, for a little while," replied Mr. Benton;

"but when you go for months this way, as we do on missionary tours, it becomes monotonous."

"Isn't everything nice and clean?" Bessie noticed. "The mats are so white, the paper on the doors is so clear of dirt, and everything looks as if it had just been scoured."

"Yes," Mr. Anson said, "the Japanese are a cleanly people, and when we get into the interior, as we go overland to Kioto, we shall have more opportunities of seeing it."

Just then the waiters came in, bringing some covered bowls upon lacquered trays.

"Where are the knives, forks, and spoons?" cried Bessie, in dismay, as a tray with the bowls upon it was set before her. "Are we to eat with our fingers? Why, what are these two sticks for? They look just like two lead-pencils, only that they have not been cut apart."

"These are chop-sticks," Mr. Benton remarked; "and they are not spilt apart so that you may know that nobody has ever eaten with them before."

"Must we eat with them?" said Bertie, in a surprised tone, to Mr. Granger.

"Yes; that is what they are for."

When they uncovered the bowls, they discovered some soup in one, a bit of fish in another, one was empty, and in another was something that they did not recognize as having ever seen it before. Mr. Anson was looking at it rather suspiciously, when Mr. Benton remarked:

"That is *chawan mushi;* it is a kind of custard; you put in your chop-sticks, and you may pull out almost any sort of an eatable."

"Yes," said Bertie, attempting a joke; "a Japanese hash."

The waiter girls, who remained in attendance, squatted upon their heels at one side, were looking with curious gaze at the attempts of the party to use the chop-sticks. Mr. Granger and Mr. Benton had no difficulty; but the rest seemed in danger of going away hungry. After laughing about it, and after a number of mishaps, owing to their clumsiness, Mr. Benton said, as he opened his satchel:

"I expected this, and so I asked my wife to put in here some such tools as you are accustomed to use," and he handed them each a fork and a spoon. "Now you will like that rice better, I think," he continued, "if you will put a little of this sugar and condensed milk upon it."

And it did improve it very greatly. After considerable merriment, the luncheon was finished, the bill was paid, and the *jin-riki-shas* turned towards Shiba.

After uncountable twistings and turnings, they stopped before a gigantic red gateway, two stories high. Passing through this, on foot, the American visitors walked slowly up an avenue, on either side of which were shrines and priests' residences. In one of these shrines, an old shaven-headed woman was in attendance. Bessie said to her mamma, that she thought she was "one of the sweetest-faced old ladies" she had ever seen.

Around the walls were hung a great many scrolls, and, as the old lady said to Mrs. Anson, through Mr. Granger, they had hundreds more very valuable ones in the chests about the shrine. A little beyond this, a bulletin-board was erected, upon which shingles, covered with Chinese characters, were placed.

"Why, what is that?" asked Bertie.

"That," said Mr. Benton, "is the way the Japanese have of publishing the names of the givers of money towards the new temple, and the amount they give. There is the Emperor's name for a thousand dollars, and they run down from this to sums of ten dollars."

Just here, the noise of tiny hammers, beating upon small anvils, was heard, and a humming sound as of a number of voices repeating something in concert. Turning to the building from whence the sound came, and after taking off their shoes, lest they should soil the clean mats, they found themselves in an oblong building, in the midst of an audience of men, women, and children. Beyond a railing, in front of the audience, upon a high pulpit, squatted a priest, with a round, jolly face. The people before him were repeating a prayer, "*Nam-nam-nam-nam*," for several minutes thus, and then suddenly bursting forth, under the priest leadership with, "*Namu Amida Butsee*,"—meaning, Hear, O Salvation-Bringing Buddha. All the while some old ladies—the choir, Bertie called them—were beating with little mallets upon metal drums before them, keeping the time of the *nam-nams*. Then of a sudden, the praying ceased, and the shaven-headed priest began to preach. He occasionally told stories which made the people laugh, and sometimes he spoke very earnestly. His sermon was a very short one. When it was over, a number of attendant priests came forward and began to pray and prostrate themselves before an idol, which was then uncovered. The whole ceremony seemed to consist in the repetition of phrases—in Sanskrit and Chinese, as Mr. Benton remarked, and which not even the priests understood. After the service was ended, some of the younger priests came nearer our friends, to see, particularly, the lady and the little girl, who were greater strangers than the gentlemen. Mr. Benton made use of the opportunity to ask the priests if they really understood their worship, and to try to tell them something about Christianity. In leaving the building, slipping his hand into his pockets, he brought forth some tracts called, "The Story of the Cross," written in the Japanese characters, and gave them to the priests and people, who received them with many expressions of thanks.

Bertie had been listening while Mr. Benton was speaking, and had noticed all his actions. Of course, he could not understand a word that was said, but he read in Mr. Benton's face and in the tones of his voice, that he was earnestly pleading with them for something, and the word

Yésu, which he could distinguish every once in awhile, made him feel certain that Mr. Benton was talking of Jesus. It was done so quietly, so simply, and so courteously, that no one seemed in the least offended, not even the priests.

"H'm," said Bertie, "Mr. Benton's a good missionary, anyhow. I wonder if they are all like him."

Beyond the preaching hall, the new temple stood. It was a square structure, having a high, curving roof, supported by immense timbers.

"Is it not top-heavy?" asked Mr. Anson.

"No," replied Mr. Benton; "the Japanese believe that buildings constructed in this way better stand the shocks of the earthquakes, which are here so frequent. Do you notice this beautiful wood? Smell these chips; is not the odor delightful? This is the *hinoki,* the 'sun-wood,' literally; and this hard, heavy timber is the *keyaki,* a kind of elm. And here is some camphor wood; notice how strong the odor of the camphor is in these newly cut chips. Do you see how the timbers are so pinned together, with wooden pegs, that some of them can sway just a little? These tiles for the roof are made of clay, and are quite heavy also. In that little room right in the centre of the rear end of the building is to be the *sanctum sanctorum*, the shrine for the idol-god. Do you notice that they are making it fire-proof, so that the idol cannot be burned up if the temple should get on fire again? Is it not strange that the Japanese should worship an idol who cannot keep himself from being burnt? But we must go to the Tycoons' Temples, where you can see one of the most beautifully finished temples in Japan. While we are walking across to one of these temples, I will tell you about their history.

"From 1616 A. D., to 1872 A. D., the rightful rulers of Japan, the *Mikados*, or Emperors, were hidden away in their palaces at Kioto, while usurpers, called the *Shōguns*, or *Tycoons*, were the real rulers of Japan. These *Shōguns* were zealous Buddhists; the greatest of the *Shōguns*, Iyé-yasŭ, took one of the sects of the Buddhists under his protection, and removed their chief monastery to this place. Here, between 1596 and 1623, the great temple was built. Yonder gateway, which we came through, has been standing since 1623. As each of the *Shōguns* died he was buried either here in Shiba, or in Uyéno, or at the town of Nikko, far to the north. The tombs themselves are very plain structures, but before each tomb a magnificent temple was built; all of these are among the marvels of Japanese art. Now we must ask this old priest to let us in."

After a few minutes of talk, the party stepped to a side door, where they removed their shoes, and proceeded to follow their priestly guide. Within, all seemed gloomy and dismal, until the priest threw open the doors at one side of the temple and let in a flood of sunlight. Then they stood in the midst of a blaze of gold. The elaborate sculptures, the brilliant coloring, the delicate metal work, dazzled their eyes with their brilliant beauty. The building was T shaped, with the top of the T towards the front, and the shrines well in the rear.

"In ancient days, before the Mikado was restored," continued Mr. Benton, "the priests sat in the front apartment, the Tycoon's family just in front of them, and up near the shrines only the High Priest ever went. To-day very little reverence is paid to the temples; the people are discouraged from coming to them, for political reasons, as one can readily see. The foreigner even—who used to be hated in Japan—can now go where formerly only the High Priest dare venture. You notice the ceiling's gorgeous paneling. See also that great piece of carving; how perfect in all its parts! Yet it is all made from one long timber. Observe the lacquer work; how hard and smooth and glossy it is."

"What are in those boxes?" asked Bertie.

"The sacred books. Let us look at them; for the priest will allow us."

So Mr. Benton opened one of the oblong boxes, and took out a roll tied with silken cords. In Chinese characters, beautifully written, they saw the sacred Buddhist books. The whole temple was beautifully finished in all its parts, too beautiful to find words to describe it. The only ugly things—ugly in foreigners' eyes—were the dragons, the griffins, the lions, and other animals that were painted on the walls.

From this temple they passed around among the tombs, out under the grand old trees, by other temples scarcely less magnificent than the one they had visited. These temples are, in reality, kept more as works of art than for use in worship. Finally as the sun was beginning to set, the group passed away to the depot, and were soon flitting along the shores of Yedo Bay, towards Yokohama.

The next day was the Lord's Day; and, escorted by Mr. Benton, who called for them early in the morning, Mr. Anson and his family climbed up the "Bluff" to the mission chapel, anxious to get a chance to see how the native Christians worshiped. The chapel was a small building, which would seat about a hundred and fifty people; it had paper windows and a matted floor. A tiny organ stood in front, at which one of the missionary ladies was seated, while the preacher, a native Japanese, was seated on one side of the table that served as a pulpit, and by his side the white-haired, veteran missionary, who, for ten years or more, had labored to give to the Japanese the gospel of Jesus Christ, as he had labored in another land for nearly a quarter of a century, to give it to another heathen people.

The order of the services was just the same as in Mr. Anson's church at Alton, though altogether in the Japanese language. Bertie and Bessie held between them a hymn book, in which the hymns had been written out in the same kind of letters used in English books, so that, after listening to a verse or two in silence, they were able to join in singing "Jesus, lover of my soul" in its Japanese translation. There was no other part of the service that they could understand; and so they watched the face of the preacher and studied their neighbors, who were giving devout attention to the sermon.

"How earnest he is!" thought Bertie. "How bright and quick his mind seems to be! I guess that he thoroughly believes all that he says. Why, this must be the man of whom Mr. Benton was telling papa, who is such a good scholar, and who chooses rather to be a Christian preacher, on poor pay, than to get a good situation under Government. I wonder why that old gentleman wanted to come away off here, when he was as old as he was; he must have cared a great deal about making these people Christians. Mr. Benton said that Dr. Browning was not going to America ever, he guessed; that he is going to stay here until he dies. Well, he must be a good man. I guess that the purser did not know such men as the doctor when he talked against missionaries."

The service being at an end, many of the

Japanese were introduced to Mr. Anson and his family by Dr. Browning and Mr. Benton; and some of them could speak the English very well. The Sunday-school here began; and Mr. Benton, with the Ansons, left to attend service in English, in the Union Church, in the settlement. Here they seemed almost at home again. If it had not been for some Japanese who sat near them, and for some red-coats from the British men-of-war, as well as some sailors from the American vessels, they would have fancied themselves back in America.

CHAPTER IV.

A JIN-RIKI-SHA JAUNT TO THE IDOL, DAI BUTZ.

THERE are very few carriage-roads in Japan, but a great many bridle-paths. Horses and carriages cannot, therefore, go very far in any direction. There are a few dozen miles of railway, all told, and many more miles projected. Mr. Anson and his party determined upon following the Tokaido, the road from Tokio—or rather from the point where the Yokohama road joins the Tokaido—to Kioto; Tokio being the "Eastern Capital" and Kioto the "Western Capital." They might have taken one of the sidewheel ocean steamers which the Japanese "Three Diamonds" Steamship Company purchased from some Americans, and have gone around by sea to Kobé, and thence up to Kioto by railroad; but this would have been a monotonous journey. The Tokaido is the road over which, until recent times, the princes and their retainers were accustomed to travel in coming to Tokio. Japan was opened to the western world by Commodore Perry in 1853, and, many years passed before it was absolutely safe for foreigners to travel in the interior. Bertie had been reading in one of the books of Japan, of the murder of Mr. Richardson on the Tokaido in 1862, and felt a little nervous when his father announced that they would follow the Tokaido to Kioto, turning off on the way to visit the gigantic idol of Dai Butz. But he was reassured when Mr. Benton told him how that murder took place. The Daimio, or Prince of Satsuma, was coming to Tokio with his train. The Japanese are a proud, haughty race, and when the foreigner and his companions, instead of turning aside for the procession to pass, sought to force their horses right through the crowd, the Japanese felt that their Prince was insulted, and so attacked Mr. Richardson. Two American gentlemen and an English lady, who had stopped at one side of the road, and who politely permitted the procession to pass them, were not harmed.

The *jin-riki-shas*, of which the travelers had already had some experience in Tokio, and by which they were to travel to Dai Butz, and to the foot of the mountains, were invented by an American missionary, it is said, in 1870. The first few were imported from San Francisco; but now they are made in Japan, where over a hundred thousand are in use. They are two-wheeled, covered carriages, with springs, holding one person comfortably, and drawn by men. Except when ascending a hill, they go at the rate of five or six miles an hour. The streets and roads are full of them, waiting to be hired at a cost of less than ten cents an hour. The men will take you from Yokohama to Dai Butz, and back—a distance of eighteen miles each way—in the same day, for seventy-five cents. All labor is cheap in Japan, and a jinriki's wages are counted to be very good indeed.

Sending their trunks around by steamer, they carried with them only the clothing absolutely needed, and some biscuits, canned milk, and canned meats, sugar, and some few other eatables, to add to such provision as the Japanese hotels would supply. They were detained for a little while awaiting their passports, without which they would not be permitted to travel more than twenty-five miles from any of the cities where foreigners can live. When the mail brought the passport from the American Minister, they started at once for Dai Butz.

Village after village, lying right along the road, was passed through. Occasionally they saw a peasant woman with a load of rice upon her back, which she bore to those who drew the rice through an iron comb, so threshing it from the straw. At other times they saw men beating the grain in huge mortars with great mallets, to separate the hulls from the grain.

Every little while they stopped at the wayside

tea-houses, where the coolies smoked their tiny pipes, and where the guests quaffed tea—without milk or sugar—from tiny cups. Finally the *jin-riki-shas* drew up in front of one of the large restaurants of Kamakura.

This city was the seat of government from 1192 A. D., to about 1450 A. D. There are very many old buildings here, mainly temples. While waiting for their luncheon to be prepared, under the guidance of one of the *jin-riki-sha* men, named Tahi, the visitors proceeded to explore the Temple of Hachiman. This temple has stood nearly seven hundred years, but was burned in 1828, and a new one erected. Passing up over steep, rounded bridges, Mr. Anson and the foreigners walked between two ponds covered with the large white flowers of the lotus. The main temple is painted red. In the temple is a permanent exhibition of historic treasures. Around its walls are hundreds of small idols. One large idol is that of Jizo. Once a certain soldier was condemned to be beheaded. The executioner found that he could make no impression on the man's neck, but that his sword became dented and nicked. On inquiry, it was found that the victim had concealed an image of Jizo in his queue, and, so the story goes, Jizo had protected him. Then he was pardoned, and a shrine to Jizo was erected.

After luncheon it was decided to walk to Dai Butz and back, as it was only a little more than a mile from Kamakura. But we will let Mrs. Anson tell the story of the visit to Dai Butz, and how it impressed her. She had promised the Mission Band a long letter when she had seen something which she thought would interest them, and so, while resting in the hotel at Yumoto before ascending the mountain, she carried out her promise.

"HOTEL YUMOTO,
FOOT OF HAKINE MOUNTAINS.

"MY DEAR YOUNG FRIENDS: I promised you a good long letter, and this is my first chance to keep the promise. I want to tell you about our trip to-day, from Yokohama to Dai Butz, that gigantic bronze image, whose picture you have seen in one of the Sciopticon lectures on Japan. But let me begin at the beginning. Mr. Benton sent word to Tahi to bring his carriage—*jin-riki-sha* he calls it. He does not harness a pony, for Tahi is both pony and driver; he himself is to pull the carriage, which is only a big baby-coach on two wheels. It is a long pull for Tahi, full eighteen miles from Yokohama to Dai Butz. Yokohama is all astir, early as it is, for the Japanese are always up at sunrise. The bay, just before us, is alive with the little boats which the *sendos*—boatmen I should say—are sculling toward the English steamer which came in during the night.

"We pass down through the native town and out into the country. Yes, country; but do not think of meadows of grass, of fields of waving wheat, or bending corn, of zigzag, or post-and-rail fences, of cows and horses, and pigs and geese, for there is scarcely any grass to be seen; no, not even a plot as large as that in your front yard, only some tufts here and there by the roadside, and on the dykes between the rice swamps. There are no fences, for there are neither cows, nor pigs, nor geese, and very few horses.

"The farm-houses are all gathered in villages; and, as in the Saviour's time in Palestine, the sower goes forth to sow. No fields of rice are yet to be seen, only the bare, dismal, muddy rice swamps are left. But if the low lands are now dismal, the hills are not. The green pines tower high up in the air, and the glossy green leaves of the camelia contrast with the red flowers with which almost all the winter through they have been covered. Camelias, not small, feeble, delicate, like those the gardeners grow at home, but large as the apple tree. The violets, white and blue, are showing their heads. The sparrows are twittering as they get ready for going to housekeeping; the crows coarsely cawing;

surely there are 'three times three in every tree,' and the Japanese say these cries are their plaintive love tones.

"We are not alone; the road is full of people, some in *jin-riki-shas*, but most afoot. We meet no wagons, for there are none to meet; no cars, for none run in this direction. The houses in the farming villages, with their thatched roofs and raised floors, are all open. The sliding doors, or windows, or walls—call them what you please— are removed from the three or four sides, leaving only the posts that support the roof. We can see only one piece of furniture, a chest of drawers. The *hibachi,* or fire box, with its handful of glowing charcoal, with the tiny bronze tea kettle over it on a tripod, stands in the centre of the room—the houses generally have but one room. A few mottoes taken from the Buddhist books, are hanging on the rear wall; and beside them the little god-shelf, with the idol in the centre, two vases with green leaves in either of them on each side of this, and two lamps,

The Ansons.

A JIN-RIKI-SHA.

Page 62.

saucers of oil with wicks afloat on either side of these, and, perhaps, a cup of rice and one of tea, placed there as offerings this morning. The floor is carpeted, not with Brussels nor Ingrain, but with rice-straw mats, each three feet by six feet, and two inches thick. The kitchen stove, an open stone, charcoal brazier, stands on the beaten ground in a corner, and over it a large closet, where in one half are kept the dishes, and in the other the quilts that are brought out at night and laid on the floor for sleeping on. Only these and nothing more, except the people.

"Everything is as neat and clean as can be. The woodwork is not painted, but it is washed two or three times daily. The floors of the little porches glisten; for when they are washed, a little soot is mixed with the water, and plenty of elbow-grease applied. Soap, there is none; they do not need it, and never use it. Mamma, with little baby strapped on her back under her outer garment, is busy, with both hands thus set free, sweeping or scrubbing;

obasan—or grandmother—is mending somebody's stockings, and some of the children are reading, some outside playing their favorite game of battledore and shuttlecock.

"In front of the house, the shoes, from mamma's big ones to baby's wee ones, all stand in a row just as they left them when they entered. For they sit on their heels on the floor. They spread their trays with dinner on them, on the floor; they sleep on the floor; so the floor must be kept clean, and every one goes about in his stocking feet. There are no hats hanging around; mamma never gets any spring bonnet; and Koshi never has to ask: 'Where's my hat?' for they never wear any, not even when they are little babies, and are exposed all day long to the hot sun. Their square-cut, blue cotton clothes are gathered at the waist by a girdle or sash—the girls' sashes are just 'gorgeous.' There are no bias plaitings, nor cuts, nor gores; the sleeves, long and square, are pockets as well.

"But we will leave them and go on. Now we come to a bridge, and up, up, up, then down, down, down, just like going over an arch. We pass the mountains; children come out crying:

"*'Anata ohaiyo!' 'Anata ohaiyo!'*

"This means 'good-morning, good-morning.' Then, handing us great bunches of red and pink and white and variegated camelias, they scamper off before we can thank them.

"At a tea-house, for a *tempo* apiece, we get a cup of tea and some cakes and sugar-coated beans. A *tempo* is a large oval coin of gun metal, about as heavy as a silver dollar, but worth only about four-fifths of a cent in our money. On through more rice-flats, and occasionally through fields where barley or wheat has been grown, and over more hills, through more farming villages, and we come to Kamakura—Kamakura, a city that might celebrate ten centennials, for it is over a thousand years old; and seven hundred years ago it was a most celebrated city. Old houses, old trees, old moats, with moss-covered stones, old bridges, old monasteries, old temples, whose steps have been hollowed out by the feet of the thousands of worshipers who, during these hundreds of years, have passed up and down.

"Again we stop at a tea-house for our luncheon. After taking off our shoes, we are shown to a little room in the second story, or rather a little room was made for us, for the pretty waiting-maid deftly put the paper sliding-doors in the grooves, and we are shut in. After we were rested, we again started out.

"Dai Butz is only a mile and a half away. We passed beneath great bird-rests, which are upright pillars of stone, with two stone slabs on their tops. We came to a great red gateway, fifty feet high. In compartments on either side are two gigantic red idols, a sort of Gog and Magog, the guardians of the entrance. Before the idols are wire screens, such as protect store windows; and hanging on these are mementoes of the visits of pilgrims—giants' straw-sandals, locks of hair, pictures, garments, cooking utensils, and nobody knows what all.

"But what is the man doing with the paper in his hand? He is reading something that is written on it. Now he puts it in his mouth, chews it, makes a 'spit-ball' of it, and throws it at the grating. It sticks, and he looks happy. The paper contained his prayer, and because it adhered to the wire grating, he thinks his prayer has been heard by the gods. If it had fallen to the ground, he would have thought that the gods would not hear him.

"Just now the road seemed to end in a clump of trees. But we followed the road, and there— beautiful! wonderful!—there, right before us— and we have not been permitted to see it until just the right moment for getting in the best position to perceive its beauty—there sits Dai Butz on the lotus lily. There he has sat, as he sits to-day, for six hundred years, without shelter from sun, or wind, or rain, or snow, or earthquake; not some ugly, hideous monster, but the beautiful idol, Dai Butz, with face turned to the ocean—the great Pacific, which stretches away for five thousand miles, until its waters wash the shores of America—as though looking for the coming of the ships that are to bring those who shall destroy his worship—there sits the bronze image of the Great Buddha. The name is made up of Dai, great, and Butz, Buddha. He is sitting in Oriental style, upon his heels; his thumbs are brought together; the head is bent forward; and the eyes fastened upon the thumb nails. The position is a fixed, easy one, nothing strained or unnatural. The features, the limbs, the drapery, are in perfect proportion, and in perfectly natural arrangement. Behind and beyond, the hills come sloping down, and are always clothed with green, and furnish a beautiful background for the beautiful idol.

"The idol is not without expression. On the contrary, it is all expression, and expressive of one great thought—it teaches the one great lesson of Buddhism. The 'pose,' the expression, indicate contemplation, or active unconsciousness, self-absorption. Buddha is wrapt in thought. We need no guide to tell us of its meaning. And it is all on so gigantic a scale—fifty feet high. Who cast it, who designed it, who was its artist architect, no one can tell. He is gone, forgotten; but his work remains. But our enchantment is broken. We are reminded that it is, after all, an idol, as we are jostled by the white-clad pilgrims, who come bowing again and again, mumbling over their prayers. Sad, sad, sad! We, too, draw nearer.

"Even when looked at closely, there is no coarseness about the idol; the bronze plates are joined evenly, and time has scarcely marked it, except to mellow and enrich its color. The bronze has more gold mixed in the alloy than bronzes usually have. We entered the idol—for it is both an idol and a temple—a window in the back lets in the light. We climbed up steep steps, and stood on a level with his chin. Idols small and great, idols handsome and ugly, idols grotesque and hideous, idols of stone and of wood, idols of bronze and of gilt, idols of all sorts and shapes and sizes, are arranged around its interior. Other foreigners have been here before us, and some have left their marks, their autographs. One vandal has printed, in large black letters, on the breast of a beautiful gilt image of Kwanon, the 'Queen of Heaven,' WEBB.

"I hope that you are keeping up your reading on missions, and that you are following us in our journeys with your loving prayers.

"Affectionately yours,

"MARGARET ANSON."

It was rather a difficult task for Mrs. Anson to get her letter finished, as every once in awhile the sliding doors would be moved aside by some curious Japanese, anxious to see the foreign lady and her little girl. But we will return to the arrival of our friends at the Hotel Yumoto.

CHAPTER V.

OVER THE MOUNTAINS TO KIOTO.

THE hotel at Yumoto, and its surroundings, were delightful. On one side rose the mountains in all their grandeur, and on the other flowed a sparkling creek. As the hotel-life along the road is very much the same as at Yumoto, we may as well take a peep at the tired travelers here as in any of the hotels along the Tokaido to Kioto.

"Would you like a bath?" was the first question asked by Dr. Olden, who had joined the travelers a little way back, and who was going on a missionary tour on the other side of the mountains.

"Yes," said Mr. Anson, immediately. "Yes, indeed, for I am very tired and dusty."

"But I think I had better tell you about the hotel baths in Japan, so as to prepare you for what may be before you. Just here I think we can make an arrangement with the landlord, by which our party can have the exclusive use of one of the baths for a few hours, so that we can go in one by one."

"Why," said Bertie, "how do you go?—by twos?"

"Yes, and sometimes by dozens. The commonest bath you will find is a box three feet square and two feet deep, filled with hot water. It is a bath, not baths, remember. About three or four o'clock in the afternoon, the tub is filled, and a charcoal fire is built in the little stove let into one side of the tub. When the water is hot, notice is given to the favored guest, who takes his bath; when he is done, another steps in, and so they go on until late in the evening. Sometimes forty or fifty people use the same bath—the same water. In Yumoto, and some other places, the baths are larger, six or seven feet square; and there are several of them. The hot water comes in an incessant stream from the bowels of the earth; it is boiled in Mother Nature's kettle. Of course, the water is always changed."

Dr. Olden saw the landlord, and after a little parleying and the promise of an extra *chadai,* or a fee, one of the baths was shut off by sliding doors, and it was reserved for the foreign guests. When they were through with their baths, they all voted them the best baths they had ever tried. The minerals of the hot waters seemed to extract all the weariness from their bodies. After a light supper—light because there was no very substantial food to be had—all prepared for bed. A screen was run through the room, giving the choicest section to Bessie and her mamma, while the gentlemen and Bertie slept in the adjoining room, which was screened off by papered sliding doors. There were no bedsteads, no hair mattresses, no feather pillows, nor yet any blankets. Two quilts were doubled up; sheets, which the guests had brought with them, and which were plentifully dusted with flea-powder, were spread over the quilts. A quilt was rolled up for a pillow, and traveling-rugs were used for coverings. After family worship, all turned in, and soon the "melody of the purling brook," as the doctor called it, lulled them to sleep.

Soon after daylight the hotel was alive again; the guests ate their breakfast hurriedly, so as to get an early start for the climb up the mountains. A basket chair, slung from a pole, to be carried on the shoulders of two coolies, was secured for Mrs. Anson, and one for Bessie. The rest preferred to walk. The road was built hundreds of years ago. Gigantic *cryptomeria* line the way. Up, up they clambered over the huge round bowlders with which the road is paved—save the mark! The ascent was, in some places, wonderfully steep, almost at an angle of forty-five degrees. They climbed three thousand feet before they reached the top; then came a slight descent of three or four hundred feet, and they reached Hakoné, twelve and a half miles, in five hours. The air was so bracing and pure, that they felt as if they had scarcely climbed at all.

They determined to go to *O Jigoku* in the afternoon. *O Jigoku* means, literally, Great Hell; that is the proper name, the name given by the Japanese a century or more ago. After a boat ride on Hakoné Lake, they commenced another climb of a thousand feet. As they neared the place to which they were going— and the way was exceedingly difficult—vegetation ceased, and the odor of sulphur was perceptible. The guide now went in advance, carefully testing the way, to see if it would bear them. They could hear, as they entered the place, the boiling of the water but a few feet beneath them. Soon they were able to see the steam arising from various vent holes, and, after a little, could see the water itself, boiling and bubbling, and casting off its sulphury odor. All around lay masses of sulphur. The ground, in places, was so soft that they could thrust their Alpine stocks almost through the crust. It was a really dangerous place, and they did not tarry very long there. The Japanese had, fittingly, one might think, placed an image of the God of Hell, Yema, in the midst of the *Solfatara*. They took a bath at the foot of the hill, in hot water, strongly impregnated with sulphur, and returned to the hotel at Hakoné. After a supper on delicious mountain trout, which Dr. Olden cooked, they tumbled into bed. They were not in a hurry to get up the next morning, as all ached more or less.

Since Dr. Olden would have to remain in Hakoné for a day or two, to attend a quarterly meeting of the native Christians of this district that was to be mainly a business meeting, he offered to find a guide for Mr. Anson and Bertie to take them to Atamiour, the mountains by the sea. Just then some Japanese urchins began to cry out, "*Ijin-san, ijin-san,*" "Foreigners, foreigners." Dr. Olden looked to see who it was, and recognized two gentlemen of his acquaintance, merchants in Yokohama. They had been a little way from the village of Hakoné on a fishing expedition, and had set out this morning to find a guide to take them to Atami. All were agreed that it was a very fortunate meeting. Soon all were ready for the start. Mrs. Anson and Bessie stood in front of the hotel and watched the travelers until they were out of sight. For the rest of the journey, I cannot do better than to quote from Mr. Anson's letter to Deacon Root, since he wrote it very soon after the exciting trip over the hills:

"A few days ago we planned to visit Atami-by-the-sea, a place famed for its hot sea-water baths, impregnated with sulphur, and for a spouting geyser. It was a fifteen-mile walk up and down the mountains. There were three ranges to be crossed. The narrow foot-path wound around as near to the tops of the mountains as possible, yet there was much going up and down. I judge that there was a descent of about five thousand feet and two thousand feet of ascent in going to Atami.

"Our plan, at starting, was not very definite. Our guide assured us that it was not a long walk to Higanesan, from whose tops ten provinces of Japan can be seen; and we thought that, perhaps, we should return from there and not go to Atami. But when we got there, we determined to go on. We reached Atami at four, took a bath, and ate our dinner. While engaged in this, the wind shifted and the clouds began to gather thickly. We had eaten leisurely, as we had concluded to stay all night at Atami, even without our luggage. The wiser ones shook their heads now, though, and declared that, if it rained, it would be a tremendous task, and a dangerous one, to climb the wet and slippery mountain paths. To go back at night seemed the smaller evil. Our guide, who had lost his way once during the afternoon, declared that he was now sure of his way, and that he would prepare torches for us. So we made up our minds to go. If we could get up to the top of the first mountain, a climb of over three thousand feet, we could get our torches at an old temple there.

"We marched off, in Indian file, on a steady tramp. Quickly the hill was left beneath us, then the mountain, and just as it began to be quite dark, we saw the temple before us. We quaffed some hot tea while our guide was getting ready the torches. The torches were made of bamboo grasses, tied tightly together; they were about six feet long, and six inches in diameter.

"But we were doomed to be disappointed. When we were on the mountain top, the wind fairly howled about our ears; to carry a torch lighted was out of the question. We were all lightly clad for walking; so when we rested to take breath, we crouched down behind a rock, or sat in some hollow in the path. Fortunately, Mr. S—— had been accustomed to following trails in the woods of the Adirondack Mountains when off hunting. Our guide could not help us in the least; he was perfectly bewildered; so we installed Mr. S—— as leader. He saw the path; we only saw his white canvas shoes. There were many dangerous portions of the road, where the path lay close beside precipitous places. We came safely by all these, however, thank God! We could not yet light our torches; the wind was too strong, though it seemed to be dying away, and we were getting into the protection of trees. Finally, we could go on no longer, and flung ourselves upon the ground in a sheltered place, and took some refreshment in the shape of crackers and raspberry jam. There was a solitary bottle of water. How good our luncheon tasted! It seemed to put new life into us.

"Off we started again; now with our guide holding his lighted torch, going in advance. One of us followed close after him, acting as pilot, calling out: 'Look out!' 'step up!' or 'step down!' 'slippery place!' 'root!' 'water!' and the like. It was quite serious business, I assure you. So for awhile longer. Then we saw a light in advance. What could it be?

We were a little anxious. Finally Mr. V. called out:

"'It is our landlord and his sons come out to hunt us up.'

"We were glad to see them, indeed. In an

FUJI-YAMA.

hour, we reached the hotel, and dropped into bed for a sound sleep."

A few mornings after, the luggage was

gathered together, and after a breakfast on mountain trout and biscuits, the descent of the mountains was commenced. Since it was so gradual and easy, even Mrs. Anson and Bessie walked. A little more than half-way down the mountain road they came to the Fuji-viewing Terrace, whence a grand view of the sacred mountain, Fuji-yama, is to be obtained. For a day or two they were to travel around the base of this mountain, which rises to a height of fourteen thousand feet above the sea level. Pilgrims were constantly met, clad in their white robes, and with little bells tied to their girdles, indicating that they had made the ascent of Fuji-yama, and their banners showed that they belonged to the sect of "Sons of Fuji."

At the foot of the mountains *Bashas*, a kind of diligence carriage, were taken. Away across the paddy-swamps, where the rice was being cultivated, or through the tea-gardens, now up slight hills, now along by the sea-shore, away they sped. Day by day passed by, each full to the brim with gladsome enjoyment, until the city of Kioto came in sight.

Just on the outskirts of Kioto, when pausing at a tea-house for a rest, Bertie, who had wandered a little further on the road to stretch his

FLOWING INVOCATION.

limbs, came to a small stream of water running by the road-side, in the middle of which was a cloth suspended at the corners upon four bamboo sticks, with a dipper resting in it.

"What can this be for?" thought Bertie.

Just then several Japanese peasants came by, stopping, however, long enough to dip up some water, and each poured a ladleful upon the cloth, letting it run through. While Bertie's bewilderment was increasing, a young Japanese, dressed in foreign clothes, stopped to rest under a tree; and, instead of the usual *Ohaiyo*, said "Good-morning."

"Do you speak English," asked Bertie.

"Yes, I am studying in the mission-school in Kioto."

"Can you tell me what that is for?"—pointing to the cloth and dipper.

"That is the *Nagaré Kanjo*, the *Flowing Prayer*. Our people believe that when a mother dies while giving birth to a child she goes into hell. She must stay there until this cloth wears out and the water no longer drips through, but runs in a steady stream; then her soul is delivered from hell. But often the priests sell a tough cloth to poor people who cannot pay much, and a thin, worn cloth to the rich."

"What a shame!" said Bertie.

"Yes, it is; but the people are learning the priests' tricks, and soon every one will see that these deceivers are seeking their own good, and not the good of the nation; and it will help to do away with our old heathen faith."

Just here the party came up, and paused long enough to listen to Bertie's story of the Flowing Invocation. Then, courteously thanking the Japanese student, they passed on towards the sacred city.

CHAPTER VI.

THE SACRED CITY OF KIOTO.

WHAT Jerusalem is to the Jews, and Benares is to the Hindus, and Mecca is to the Mohammedans, is Kioto to the Japanese. To tell all that Bertie and Bessie saw while in Kioto, would fill a volume. Just before they sailed from Kobé, below Kioto, for China, they were talking over that which had struck them most forcibly in their visit to Kioto. Bessie thought that she would remember longest the view of the city from the mountains east of Kioto, to which they had one day climbed; but Bertie thought that he would never forget their visit to the mission-school and theological seminary, and their afternoon in the great Temple of Nishi-Hongwanji. But we will go back to their entrance to the town.

Passing by several hotels, wearied and tired from the long *jin-riki-sha* ride, and anxious to reach a resting spot, they finally drew up before the Mariyama Hotel, the place where foreigners generally stop when in Kioto. When Dr. Olden left them at Shidzūōka, he had employed for Mr. Anson as a guide, a young man named Sasaki, who spoke English remarkably well, and who was very familiar with the country through which they were to travel. It was at Sasaki's suggestion that the Mariyama Hotel was chosen. As it was growing rapidly dark and the foreigners were very weary, they were not disposed to look farther, at any rate, and, as it turned out later, they could not have found any better hotel.

After a light supper, and a settling of accounts with the *jin-riki-sha* pullers, and a brief walk about the hotel garden, the party settled down to rest. Mr. and Mrs. Anson occupied one room, from the corner of which a part was screened off with a six-fold screen for Bessie's use, while Bertie with Sasaki occupied an adjoining room.

Sasaki watched with great curiosity while Bertie took out his pocket Testament before undressing, read for a little, and then kneeled upon the matting to pray.

"Where are your gods?" asked Sasaki.

"Why, don't you know that there is but one God, and that he forbids us to make any image of him? I thought that you, who can speak such good English, would know that," replied Bertie.

"No, I learned my English at the University, and they never said anything about the American God."

"No," added Bertie, "he is not an American God; he is the God of all nations and all worlds."

Then, as they were lying side by side, there followed a long conversation about the Christian religion. Finally, Sasaki asked Bertie to let him see his "sacred book," and on taking it he went to the lamp and began reading the first chapter of Matthew's Gospel. The frequent *Naruhodos* showed how deeply he was interested. Finally, laying down the Testament, he bent his head in thought, then taking up the Testament again, he turned back as if trying to find something he had read. Bertie was lying quietly, watching with anxious interest and waiting for Sasaki to say something. After Sasaki had found that which he was looking for, he bent over his head, laid the Testament open before him, and commenced to read in a low voice:

"Our Father which art in Heaven."

Then, as if satisfied, he laid himself down. He was very restless, as if unable to sleep. Finally, Bertie said:

"What do you think of what you read?"

"Why, I thought you were asleep."

"No, I could not go to sleep; I was anxious about you. I wish very much that you were a Christian."

"Well, I never knew anything about this.

I heard our priests, of course, saying that the Jesus religion was a bad religion, and that we should go to hell if we left our old worship and became Christians; and I never thought much about it."

"Well, you will think about it now, won't you?"

"Yes, I will."

"Will you let me make you a present of my Testament?" said Bertie. "I can easily get another when we get to Kobé."

"Yes; and I thank you very much."

This was the end of the conversation, but not the end of Sasaki's interest in Christianity. For, after they had returned to America, Mr. Anson received a letter from one of the missionaries in Kioto, saying that a few days after they had gone he happened to meet Sasaki. When he mentioned that he was a missionary, Sasaki drew out Bertie's Testament and asked if *that* was his religion. On being told that it was, Sasaki asked if he might ask some questions.

The missionary encouraged and helped him, invited him to his school and home and church; and, it resulted, after several months of patient inquiry on Sasaki's part, in his becoming a Christian.

On sliding aside the windows, the next morning, Mrs. Anson was surprised at the charming view. The grand old spreading fir-trees, the lovely garden, the richly wooded slope beyond, and between was the plain of the vast city, with its beautifully proportioned and elegantly shaped pagodas rising every here and there in and about the city. For some time she stood enjoying the scene; then calling Mr. Anson and Bessie, they sat upon the balcony and watched the scene below them. In one of the little dwellings at the foot of the hill, the doors had all been pushed aside, and the woman of the house was bustling about getting the breakfast ready. Soon she was joined by her husband and child, and they saw them stepping to one side of the room where the husband pushed aside the doors of the god-shelf, on which were some images, and below the shelf, in the recess, was hanging a scroll picture of the Seven Household Gods. Offerings were placed on the shelf, they bowed in prayer, and then turned to the morning meal. Later in the day, Bertie, at Bessie's request, bought a scroll like that in the servant's house, and another with the picture of the foremost of the Household Gods, Fukuroku Jin, the god who gives long life to his worshipers. He has a great, tall head, grown very large by thinking so much. His eyebrows and beard are white and snowy. The tortoise and the crane are Fukuroku Jin's pets. Sasaki pointed to the graceful form of the goose in the picture, and said:

"Do you know that when we Japanese wish to compliment a person, we compare him to the wild goose?"

After breakfast they went for a day's picnic to the Eastern Mountains, the Higashi Yama, for Mr. Anson thought that if they could get a bird's-eye view of the city and surrounding country, they would much more enjoy their rambles through the city and among its temples. This opinion proved correct. A magnificent prospect over town and country was spread before them. The city stretches north and south, and the streets are laid out like those of Philadelphia, in regular right angles.

Kioto has nearly three hundred thousand inhabitants, and over a thousand temples. It began to be an important place about eleven hundred years since. Away in the northern section of the city is the palace, while in the extreme south the railroad station could be plainly seen, and the railroad stretching away, a glittering thread, towards Kobé. Not far from the station, the monstrous temple of Nishi Hongwanji could be plainly seen, and other temples and pagodas scattered hither and thither.

Well on in the afternoon, the picnickers returned to the city. At the hotel they found a number of curio dealers waiting to sell to the foreigners curiosities in bronze and bamboo, in ivory and silk, works of art and ornament, as well as useful objects. By Sasaki's advice, Mr. Anson bought nothing of them, but waited until he could go out among the stores. Besides the fact that these dealers asked a much higher price than the articles were worth, they were not such as Mr. Anson wished to carry home with him.

In the early evening they took a stroll among the stores, where Mr. Anson purchased a number of discarded idols, and where he secured a large number of volumes of picture books with engravings by famous Japanese artists, chief of whom was Hokusai. The next day they had planned to visit the temple of the Hongwanji, but it rained steadily all day, so that they were kept house-bound. This gave them a chance to write up their letters, and to examine, with Sasaki's help, the picture books they had bought. Hour after hour passed rapidly away in this pleasant occupation. Sasaki had stories

DRIVING OUT DEVILS ON NEW YEAR'S EVE.

to tell concerning most of the pictures—fables, parables, and historic occurrences. The religious element of the Japanese nature appeared in almost every picture, and very much information concerning their religious views was gained from the pictures. One curious work was Hokusai's "One Hundred Views of Mount Fuji," another was his "Man Girafu," or "Ten Thousand Pictures." In one of these books, Bertie noticed a picture of a man driving the devils out of his house, on the eve of the New Year, with beans that had been blessed by the priest. This Hokusai is the most famous and most popular of all Japanese artists.

When Bertie rose the next morning, he went quickly to see how the weather might be, for one rainy day in a Japanese hotel is quite enough to tax one's patience. He was delighted to find the air wondrously pure and the sky clear, while a strong breeze was rapidly drying up the mud.

The next few days were spent in visiting the most noted temples under Sasaki's guidance.

From Kobé, Bertie wrote to his Sunday-school teacher about their visit to one of the most famous of Kioto's temples, that of the Nishi Hongwanji:

"MY DEAR TEACHER: Since we came to Kioto, I have seen so many beautiful temples and so many curious things, that I hardly know where to begin in writing to you. Before I write of our sight-seeing, I want to tell you that the young Japanese who is our guide seems interested in Christianity, and he often reads in my Testament. The day before we left Kioto, we went to the great temple of the Hongwanji. Sasaki, our guide, tells me that in the year 1262, a man named Shinran Shonin, a sort of Martin Luther, founded a sect called the Monto sect, as a protest against the ritualistic habits of some other Buddhists. The Monto sect is the most powerful sect in all Japan; some of its priests have studied in England. The Monto sect has temples in all the great cities, with vast enclosures and huge sweeping roofs.

"When we went to see this temple, we saw also the great priest, Akamatz; he spoke a few words to us in very pure English. It is a beautiful temple. The walls have golden panels, or, rather, the sliding doors are covered with gold-leaf, with pictures of birds and flowers painted upon them. The roof is held up by round pillars made of *hinoki*, or sun-wood. The altar is painted in black lacquer, the same that we see on the beautiful Japanese trays and cabinets. The shrine is very beautiful. I asked Sasaki where the idols were, and he told me that they did not have any, for the Monto sect does not believe in idol worship. Yet I remember that in the Monto Temple in Tokio they had one idol, which, we were told, was the quintessence of all the gods. It is a vast, dim, silent temple. I noticed that one flower in particular was painted on the walls, and cast in bronze; papa said that it was a lotus flower, and the priest said that it meant purity; for, as purity grows out of the filth of men's hearts, so the lotus grows out of slime and mud. Out in the gardens were many very beautiful objects, but they had nothing to do with the temple.

HIOGO BUDDHA.

"Yesterday we took a trip to Hiogo, and we saw the beautiful image of Buddha, a photograph of which I send to you in this letter.

"We often talk about home, and when we get back I shall have many things to show you and to tell you.

"Your affectionate scholar,
"BERTIE ANSON."

CHAPTER VII.

TO THE LAND OF TEAS AND QUEUES.

EARLY one morning, a day or two later, the steamer sailed from Kobé for Shanghai, China. Though the steamer would sail for some days to come within the limits of the Empire of Japan, and though the Ansons would once more set foot on Japanese soil, yet the visit to Japan was practically over. As they leaned over the stern of the steamer, watching the fast disappearing houses of Kobé, the entire family seemed to be absorbed in thought.

"I wonder if I shall ever see Japan again," said Bertie to himself. "I hope so, for I feel as if I was leaving home. I wonder how Sasaki will get along. I hope that he will become a Christian. If he does, why, may-be I have had something to do with it. Perhaps I can come back, when I get to be a man, as a missionary to Japan."

The steamer was named the Hiroshima Maru, and carried, at the mast-head, the flag of the company to which she belonged, a company composed entirely of Japanese, the Mitsu Bishi Company, whose symbol is but a translation of its name, three diamonds arranged with their points touching. The steamer was a sidewheeler, with comfortable, airy cabins; not so large nor so fast as the screw-propellers, but much more comfortable, except in severe storms.

After leaving Kobé, the steamer ploughed its way through the Inland Sea of Japan, famed for its beautiful scenery. It was like a great lake, yet, in reality, it was but an inlet of the ocean. Through the whole two hundred and fifty miles of its length, one can always see the shore, and often the steamer approaches quite close to it. Fleets of junks were passed, and once a small steamer plying between Nagasaki, Simoneseki, and Kobé. Simoneseki is at the other end of the Inland Sea, but since foreigners are not permitted to land there, it not being an open port, the Ansons had to be content with the view from the steamer's deck. But as they were to have a day and a half in Nagasaki, they did not mind the loss.

The harbor of Nagasaki is very much like the harbor of Rio Janeiro, in South America. It is a bay surrounded by wooded hills, with its mouth seaward; just in the opening, a sort of natural breakwater, lies the Island of Pappenberg.

"Have you ever heard the story of that island," asked Mr. Anson.

"It seems to me that I have heard the name, and I remember thinking that it sounded unlike a Japanese word; but I don't remember the story," said Mrs. Anson.

"Oh, tell it, papa," Bertie and Bessie asked, in the same breath.

"Suppose we wait until we get ashore, then we will climb up the hills where we can get a good view of the island, when I will tell it to you."

Since they were not encumbered with baggage, the Ansons had no difficulty in speedily getting ashore. For several hours they strolled through the narrow streets of Nagasaki, among its one-storied houses. Back from the houses, at the foot of the hill, they came to the Temple of The Ever-merciful Buddha, with its gigantic roofs.

Ascending the well-worn stone steps, they were soon inside the temple, where worship was just about to begin. Clouds of incense filled the air, and the long-drawn, oft-repeated prayer, *Namu Amida Butsee*, was heard. The people began to count the beads upon their rosaries, the priests to beat the drums, while the chief priest proceeded to raise the veil before the idol. After a little the sacred books were brought by an attendant, and a pile placed by the side of each squatting priest. Then at a signal from the chief priest, all the while intoning a prayer, the priests took up volume after volume, and began to swing the leaves open and shut, thus with each volume three times. All the while the chief priest kept tapping some bronze vases before him, with his bawble, while he intoned a prayer and threw incense upon the brazier. When all the books had been opened and shut—in their estimation, just as good as reading them all through—the veil was drawn before the shrine, and the service was over for the day. In the rear of the temple they saw an old graveyard, in which were grave-stones with the symbol of the lotus flower, and, frequently, a Sanskrit letter.

After a luncheon of fish and rice, with a few biscuits and some condensed milk, the Ansons, guided by one of the coolies, climbed the steep hill in the rear of the town. This was arranged in great steps, and was cultivated all the way to the top. From the summit a beautiful view of the city and harbor was to be had. As they settled around Mr. Anson in a group, Bertie reminded him of the promised story.

"I hardly know where to begin," said Mr. Anson; "but I judge that the best place will be the coming of St. Francis Xavier to Japan. Do you remember hearing that name before, Bertie?"

"Yes, sir; he was one of the followers of the Jesuit, Loyola, and they sometimes call him the Apostle to the Indies. Was he ever in Japan?"

"Yes, over two hundred and thirty years ago he came to Christianize Japan."

"But," interrupted Bertie, "I thought you said, papa, when we were in Tokio, that it was only about thirty years since foreigners were permitted to come to Japan."

"True enough, as to more recent times; but several hundred years ago foreigners, the Dutch and the Portuguese, in particular, were allowed to live in Japan, and to trade with the Japanese. My story is connected with both peoples, and shows how it came about that for a great many years, until 1853, in fact, foreigners were forbidden to come to Japan."

"Who forbade them, papa?"

"Why, the Japanese, of course; for they have always been their own masters. Two hundred and fifty years ago the Dutch and the Portuguese were great sailors and traders; they discovered many countries, and opened up commerce with many others already known. These two nations were rivals, and in their rivalry often said bitter words of one another. The Portuguese were the first to come to Japan, and the Dutch came not long after. The Dutch did nothing at all to Christianize the Japanese; but the Portuguese were very earnest in this work. In the year 1549, Francis Xavier came to Japan, and in thirty or forty years it was said that there were not less than five hundred thousand converts to Christianity. Some of the princes were converted, and were very zealous Roman Catholics, anxious to do almost anything to make their people, too, become Roman Catholics. The Dutch noticed the success of the Portuguese, and, in their jealousy, tried to find occasion to put a check to it. They were not long in finding a reason; for an embassy to Rome and some rather boastful declarations on the part of some of the Japanese princes, gave the Dutch a chance to suggest that the Portuguese priests were plotting to make Japan a part of the possession of the Roman Catholic Church, under the control of Portugal. Possibly there was good ground for the suggestion. At any rate, it was enough to inspire the Japanese rulers with the determination to check the progress of the Portuguese, and to utterly extinguish Christianity in Japan.

"Do you notice," continued Mr. Anson, "that the Island of Pappenberg, lying in the mouth of the bay, has one side like a precipice? Well, from that steep rock thousands and thousands of Japanese Roman Catholics were hurled to death, just because they were Christians. About this time, in the whole country, nearly a hundred thousand Christians were killed, the remainder forsaking, either really or only apparently, their Christian faith. Then an edict was issued, forbidding the people to own Bibles or to worship Jesus, under pain of death, and commanding them to trample under foot the cross and every other Christian symbol. It was only a dozen years ago that these edict-boards were taken down, though for a few years before the edict was a dead letter. We will go off to Pappenberg, if we have time to-morrow, and you can see close at hand the rock of death where so many perished."

"There is another little island of which I have read, Deshima; where is that?" asked Mrs. Anson.

"That little island, lying yonder, not far from shore, about six or seven hundred yards square, is the one you mean. When the Japanese expelled Christianity and drove out the Portuguese, they gave the Dutch permission to live on that little island. They could only leave the island once in three years to go up to Tokio. Only one ship a year was allowed to come to them in Japan from Holland. There was a bridge from the shore to the island, where Japanese soldiers always stood on guard. From that day until the American sailor, Commodore Perry, came to Japan, in 1853, foreigners have been forbidden to land in Japan."

The next day was too stormy to permit of any excursion, and the family soon sought their quarters on the steamer, which were more pleasant, on a rainy day, than the Japanese hotel on shore. The work of putting in coal continued, the almost naked coolies not minding the rain. So the vessel was ready to steam out of port in the afternoon. Generally, it takes but two days to get across from Nagasaki to Shanghai. The rain continued all night, pouring incessantly. Somewhere towards morning, the passengers were awakened by the tossing and heaving of the vessel, and—which is almost always noticed immediately when it happens—by the silence of the great engine.

"What's the matter?" called out Bessie, in distress.

"I don't know, my dear; I will get up and see," answered Mr. Anson. "You all lie still until I come back."

To lie still was no easy task, for the vessel was heaving so heavily that it threatened to spill them out of their berths. In the pantry they could hear dishes crashing. Overhead, sailors were calling to one another in hoarse tones, and the howling wind seemed almost immediately to carry away the sound of their voices. In fear and trembling, while Mr. Anson was away, Mrs. Anson and Bessie waited.

"We are in a cyclone," were Mr. Anson's first words, as, accompanied by a watchman bringing a light, he returned.

"Why don't they go on?" asked Mrs. Anson.

"Because the rolling of the ship keeps one wheel almost always out of the water, and so we could make no progress if the engine was in motion."

"Is there any danger?"

"Yes, we may get caught in the very centre of the cyclone, and then it would be all up with us. But the captain thinks that we are only in the outer edge of it; and so by laying to, we shall escape more serious damage."

"*More* serious damage? Why, what damage *is* done?"

"Two of the small boats were washed away, and, while I was looking out of the window, I chanced to glance up into the rigging. As I was looking at the sailors furling the sails, I saw one—a Japanese, I think, he must have been—when a sudden wind struck the ship, loosen his grasp and fall into the water. In a moment the waves had washed him far from help."

"Oh, horrible! and we may have to go through that!" exclaimed Mrs. Anson.

"My dear, let us remember that we are in

our Father's care, and whether we live or die, he will not forsake us. Both we and our children, thank God, are trusting in the Saviour, and death is not a dread enemy to us, since Jesus has taken away his power. But we do not expect to die yet. The captain said, as another passenger told me, that while the situation was serious, and we were in some danger, yet we shall probably come through all right."

Just then some heavy tramping was heard in the dining-room adjoining, and Mr. Anson, going out, met the first officer, who said, in answer to his question:

"Yes, we are all right now. Pretty soon we shall begin to go ahead again. It was a severe blow, and very trying on this old tub of a vessel; but we only caught the tail end of the typhoon."

Mr. Anson returned to the state-room. And, after tucking pillows under the edges of the mattresses of Bessie and Mrs. Anson, to prevent their being rolled out, climbed to his own berth, and, with a trunk strap, made himself secure.

"Well, well," thought he, "Bertie must sleep soundly; I did not hear a word from him as I passed his state-room door."

Soon the thug-thug of the engine was heard, and, while the steamer continued to pitch up and down considerably, it was easy to be seen that the motion was getting less and less violent.

In the morning, Bertie was early upon deck. The sun shone clearly, the air seemed wondrous pure, the waves ran low, and there was scarce a sign of a storm. When his father joined him, he said:

"How is it that the storm didn't awaken you, Bertie?"

"Storm, why, was there a storm? I didn't know it."

"Yes, a very heavy one."

'I dreamed that I was being tossed up in a blanket, just as we used to be at Mrs. Penrose's school, when we cut up our capers. I suppose the storm made me dream that way."

"So you slept soundly, eh, my boy," said the

captain, who had come up behind Bertie; "well, you would make a good sailor."

This day and the next passed quietly away, until towards evening, when the vessel steamed into the mouth of the Yang-tse-kiang, and an hour or so after, into the Woosung River. About two hours later they were anchored before Shanghai, and soon the Ansons had set foot upon the soil of the great Chinese Empire.

Mr. Anson secured rooms in an American Hotel in Shanghai, for he had determined, while showing every appreciation of the hospitality of the missionaries, not to thrust himself and his family upon them. Early the next morning, some of the missionaries, who had seen the notice of the arrival of the Hiroshima Maru and its list of passengers in the daily paper, called upon Mr. Anson and gave him and his family a cordial welcome to China. Mr. Anson had only vaguely outlined his visit to China, rightly judging that the missionaries could aid him with their advice. After quite a consultation with several well-traveled missionaries, he determined first to visit Pekin, the capital, and later on to visit Hong-Kong and Canton; and if the opposition to foreigners had so far subsided as to permit of it, to go up the Canton River some distance.

CHAPTER VIII.

FROM SHANGHAI TO PEKIN.

IN Shanghai the foreign population live along the river front, and the Chinese back from the river. The foreign section has separate divisions for the American, English, and French residents. The foreigners' residences are separated by neat gardens; but the Chinese crowd as closely together as possible. There is no country in the world where the people are so thickly packed together as in China, and instead of working them harm, they seem to thrive upon it.

Just as soon as possible, the Ansons paid a visit to the Chinese city of Shanghai. Bessie, in a note to one of her school friends, wrote of their first visit:

"I think this is the dirtiest city we have ever been in. The streets are narrow and dark, and not like those in Japan. The stores are only big boxes, and the people who sell to you are not at all polite. Whenever we stopped at a shop the Chinese gathered around us; and they pushed and shoved us, and laughed at us, and called us 'Fan Kwai.' Some one told us afterward that this means Foreign Devil. They were ever so much ruder than the Japanese. I am almost sorry that we came here; but papa says that we shall enjoy ourselves better the longer we stay, and the more accustomed we become to the ways of the people. One of the missionaries says that many of the Chinese call foreigners 'devils' more from habit than because they really mean it. Often, as we went along the streets, I had to hold my handkerchief to my nose, because the smell was so bad. We took some tea once in awhile, and that did not taste badly. Often we were pushed up against the walls of the houses as some 'coolies,' as they call the men who carry burdens, came along carrying some big bundles hung from the ends of a pole that rested on their shoulders. The people seem to carry almost everything in this way. I saw a 'sedan-chair' carried on the shoulders of four men; papa is going to let me ride in one some day. To-morrow we are going to Pekin."

Bertie wrote a characteristic letter concerning what he saw, to one of his chums:

"This is a funny country, I tell you. Everything is upside down and wrong end foremost. The signs read from the top to the bottom, and not from left to right, as at home. The letters are words and the words letters, and they look just like the marks on the tea-chests, and on the packages of fire-crackers. The men wear slippers with soles an inch thick, and they *blacken* their soles with *chalk*. The men wear petticoats and the women trousers. When people, meet, they shake their own hands and not one another's. The sign of respect is not to take off your hat, but to pull off your shoes. And there are ever so many queer ways of working. The 'boy'—that is what foreigners always call men servants—says in his 'pigeon English' that it is *we* who are upside down, and not the Chinese. It is funny, Bob, to hear a Chinaman talk 'pigeon English;' *pigeon* is their way of saying business. They think that this sort of talk is a sign of great learning on their part. I will copy you a few verses from a 'Chinese pigeon English' version of the poem we used to declaim at school, Excelsior:

"TOP-SIDE GALAH!"

That nightee teem he come chop-chop,
One young man walkee—no can stop;
Maskee snow, maskee ice;
He cally flag wit 'h chop so nice—
"Top-side Galah!"

He muchee solly; one piecee eye
Lookee shalp—so fashion—my;
He talkee lalge, he talkee stlong,
Too muchee culio; allee same gong—
"Top-side Galah!"

Insidee house he can see light,
And evly loom got file all light;
He lookee, plenty ice move high,
Insidee mouth he plenty cly—
"Top-side Galah!"

Olo man talkee. "No can walk,"
Bimeby lain come, velly dalk;
"Have got watel, velly wide!"
Maskee, my must go top-side—
"Top-side Galah!"

And so it goes on. Isn't it queer, that a Chinaman can't pronounce *r*, but says *l* instead, as velly for very; while a Japanese cannot pronounce *l*, but says *r* instead, as ramp for lamp. Papa brought another piece of 'pigeon English' about the Bamboo; it begins:

One piecee thing that my have got,
Maskee that thing my no can do,
You talkee you no sabee what?
Bamboo.

And so it goes on. It all sounds funny. To-morrow we are going to start for Pekin. We go by steamer up the coast, until we reach Tien tsin, near the mouth of the Peiho River. Good-bye, Bob. Remember me to all the boys."

At the mouth of the Peiho, the steamer passed the Taku forts, celebrated in the attack of the British men-of-war, in 1859. All the way up from Taku to Tien-tsin the river was crowded with junks and *sampans,* or small boats. The Grand Canal begins at Tien-tsin. Our travelers were impatient to be in Pekin, about two days' journey—about ninety miles—from Tien-tsin. So, bright and early the day after landing, Bertie and his father took ponies, and Bessie and Mrs. Anson rode in a kind of sedan-chair carried by mules. On another pony their baggage and provisions were strapped. It took nearly a day after their arrival in Pekin before the aches and pains, brought on by the two days' ride, had left them. There is a kind of carriage used in Pekin that is drawn by a horse. In summer, the Chinese put up a cover over both horse and cart.

Pekin is one of the largest cities in the world; for it has a population of about two millions. There are really two cities in one: the Tartar city and the Chinese city, separated from each other by a high wall. The whole city is surrounded by high walls, and has thirteen gates. The Chinese city has three separate enclosures, one within the other; in the outer circle are ordinary shops and dwellings; within the second are the government offices and some private resi-

TEMPLE OF HEAVEN, PEKIN.

dences; while within the heart of the city is the imperial palace and also the imperial temples. Each one of these circles has a high wall about it. The temples within the inner circle are the most splendid in all China; they are devoted to the worship of the sun, the moon, and the earth; to farming, business, and the like. The most splendid of all is the Temple of Heaven, as foreigners call it. After some difficulty and delay, Mr. Anson managed to get a special permission, admitting the family to see the temples and a part of the palace. Mr. Anson asked one of the missionaries in Pekin to write out for him a sketch of the Temple of Heaven and the worship there:

"The imperial worship of Shang-te—the Supreme Being—on the round hillock in the southern part of the enclosure is attended with all the solemnity of which such an occasion is capable. The altar is a beautiful marble structure, ascended by twenty-seven steps; a balustrade surrounds each terrace. On the upper of these three terraces are five tables, or altars, on which the offerings to Shang-te are laid. On another terrace stands the conspicuous Temple of Agriculture. On the day before the annual sacrifices at the Winter Solstice, the Emperor goes to the Hall of Fasting. Here he spends the night in watching and meditation, after first inspecting the offerings. There are no images here, nothing but tablets. The southern altar, the most important of all Chinese religious buildings, is on a triple circular terrace, two hundred and ten feet across at the base, and ninety feet across at the top. The terraces are between five and six feet high. The temple itself is a three-storied structure, just ninety-nine feet high. The roofs are covered with tiles of a sky-blue color. At the time of sacrificing, the tablets to Heaven and to the Emperor's ancestors are placed on an altar within the temple. The Emperor kneels upon the central stone of a platform of nine marble flags, so he seems to himself and his court—while in the very centre of the central Temple of the central ('Middle') kingdom, of the central planet—to be in the very centre of the universe. By kneeling, he acknowledges that he is inferior to Heaven, and to Heaven alone. Sacrifices are offered to the dead ancestors, but to Heaven ('Shang-te') is offered a piece of blue jade stone, about a foot long, as a symbol of sovereignty. A whole burnt offering is also sacrificed to Heaven."

Confucius has some temples in the neighborhood of the Temple of Heaven. He was the religious-political reformer who lived about five hundred years before Christ, just a century later than Daniel. He was held in high repute for his wonderful wisdom, and his books are yet studied, as containing the very cream of wisdom. Nobody can have a place in ruling the country except he first successfully passes an examination in the writings of Confucius. Bertie heard from some of the missionaries some very curious stories of Chinese school-boys. Here are one or two:

About twelve hundred years ago there lived a boy named Lei Peh, who, while he was yet young, left school and started for home. On the road he saw an old woman engaged in grinding an iron pestle. Peh asked her what she was doing. She replied, "I want to make a needle." The reply touched him, and he turned back to school, and applied himself until he had mastered the classics of Confucius. Another lad, Sie Ma Wan by name, was accustomed to use a round block of wood for a pillow. When he became too sleepy, his pillow would roll, and then he would be awakened and would apply himself to his studies with vigor. Another boy, named Kwang Hung, was so poor that he could not afford a light by which to study. He bored a hole through the partition, and so let in a few rays of light from his neighbor's candle. With such stories as these the Chinese encourage the boys to study the sacred books of Confucius.

While rambling around, apart from the rest of the folks, Bertie came upon some strange objects fixed in posts, or lying upon small tables. Every once in awhile a priest would set them a whirling and then go on his way; and another passing priest would do the same. One of these was in a little porch. It consisted of a wooden drum, covered with leather. Upon the leather, strange characters were written. Bertie saw that they were not Chinese characters. The leather was stained and dirty, as if it had been much handled. Seeing him curiously examining it, one of the priests, a bright, jolly looking man,

PRAYING MACHINE.

came and said, in broken English:

"You Melican boy, you sabee dis? You no sabee? Dis allee same makee pray."

Here he put his hands together and looked up toward the sky.

"Oh, I see," said Bertie; "you mean this is a praying machine."

"Yes, yes," replied the priest.

"What this?" asked Bertie, pointing to the writing on the leather.

"That number one good prayer," and turning it as he spoke and pointing to the words, "*Om mani padmi hum.*" "Dis no Chinee language; dis writing of—what you say?—Ind—Ind——"

"India," added Bertie; "you mean old language of India?"

"Yes, old language, long time ago makee speakee, makee writee."

"What is this?" asked Bertie, taking up one of the praying-wheels which was to be turned in the hand.

"Dat allee same good prayer. Sposee man turn one time good, one hundred time better, one thousand times he number one good man, go to Joss [he meant to be with God] sure."

Several weeks were spent in and about Pekin. Every day seemed to bring something new to notice. The dusty, narrow streets were always crowded with people; and Pekin seemed, to our travelers, more noted for its foul odors than even Cologne with all the stenches of which Coleridge speaks. Pekin is an ideal Chinese city. Foreign influence has but little affected it; Chinese manners and customs are most easily studied here. The immense crowds of people, and of all classes, constantly thronging its highways and byways, are a far more interesting study than any sort of buildings or works of art.

CHINESE PRAYING-WHEEL.

The street scenes of such a city are most worthy of notice. Trades are rarely pursued in-doors; even if they are, the fronts of the shops are all open, so that the interior is exposed to view. Generally the mechanic plies his business in the streets, and goes about from place to place seeking his customers. Money-changers and musicians, pipe-sellers, and old clothes' dealers, basket-makers, lantern-sellers, and almost every other calling, jostle one another in the crowded and narrow and noisy streets. The cities are so many bee-hives; the buzzing keeps up from early morn until late at night, day after day, almost the year round. The Chinese mechanic knows no day of rest. An occasional feast-day, or a national holiday, or an hour snatched now and then to hasten to the temples, is all of the rest he takes. It is a tread-mill existence, with precious little enjoyment to ease its wearisome plodding. Religion, such as they have, offers to the Chinese no relief here, and little promise of any hereafter. There is no hope for happiness, or a respite from exacting toil, for the

PAGODA OF TUNG-CHO.

Chinese workingman. The little children even seem like old folks; the merry, joyous light of youth dies down very early in life. Wherever the religion of Jesus Christ gets a grasp on the heart, at once there comes a lifting up, notwithstanding that becoming a Christian is sufficient to subject the convert to persecution. This was most apparent to our friends when they met on the Lord's Day in one or another of the mission churches of Pekin. Of course, they could not understand a word that was spoken, but it was easy to see the difference between the spirit of the worship here and that in the temples.

On one Monday morning, with some missionary friends, the Ansons paid a visit to the Pagoda of Tung-cho, an hour or two from Pekin. A pagoda is, properly, a relic-house—a high structure, generally solid, built over the relics of some dead Buddhist saints. In China, the many-storied towers erected in temple grounds are generally called pagodas. The one at Tung-cho has thirteen stories, and is one hundred and fifty feet high, and one hundred and twenty feet around the base. It can be seen miles away from the city. Lighted lanterns are often hung at the corners of each story's roof, and little bells swing from the angles.

It was of the Porcelain Pagoda of Nankin—whose sides and roofs were covered with yellow, green, red, and white glazed porcelain tiles—that Longfellow wrote in his "Keramos." Standing beneath the pagoda at Tung-cho, one of the missionaries recited the lines:

> And yonder by Nankin, behold!
> The Tower of Porcelain, strange and old,
> Uplifting to the astonished skies
>   Its nine-fold painted balconies,
> With balustrades of twining leaves,
> And roofs of tile, beneath whose eaves
>   Hang porcelain bells that all the time
> Ring with a soft, melodious chime;
> While the whole fabric is ablaze
>   With varied tints, all fused in one
> Great mass of color, like a maze
>   Of flowers illumined by the sun.

Unfortunately, this beautiful pagoda was destroyed by the Tai Ping rebels in 1860.

CHAPTER IX.

THE STORY OF "CHINESE GORDON."

WHILE the Ansons were yet in Pekin, the mail brought up from Shanghai papers containing the latest news from Egypt, with especial reference to the dangerous position of General Gordon in Khartoum. Every now and then the party had been coming upon ruined buildings and the like, which had been destroyed by the Tai Ping rebels. This led Bertie frequently to ask his papa about the Tai Pings. But Mr. Anson knew scarcely more than his son. Fortunately, they were invited one evening to take dinner with a veteran missionary and his family. The occasion was too good a one to be lost; and at the first opportunity Mr. Anson began to lead his host to speak of his past life. A reference to Gordon and the Tai Pings brought out from the old missionary an exceedingly interesting account of Gordon's life in China, especially as to the missionary's own personal acquaintance and interviews with Gordon.

"It was in September of 1860," said Dr. Hoddard, "that I first saw Gordon. I happened to be in Tien-tsin then. It was at the time when the French and English were advancing upon Pekin. Gordon was then a captain under Sir Hope Grant. Pekin was taken on October 12. A picture of the civilization of China is given in Gordon's letter, written after the destruction of Pekin's famous palaces:

"'We (*i. e.*, our armies) went out, and after pillaging it, burned the whole place, destroying, in a vandal like manner, most valuable property, which could not be replaced for four millions (of pounds, equal to twenty millions of dollars). You can scarcely imagine the beauty and magnificence of the places we burned. The palaces were so large, and we were so pressed for time, that we could not plunder them carefully.

Quantities of gold ornaments were burned, considered as brass. Everybody was wild for plunder. You would scarcely conceive the magnificence of this residence (the Summer Palace), or the tremendous devastation the French have committed. The throne and room were lined with ebony, carved in a marvelous way. There were huge mirrors of all shapes and kinds, clocks, watches, musical boxes, magnificent china of every description, heaps and heaps of silks of all colors, embroidery, and as much splendor and civilization as you would see at Windsor; carved ivory screens, coral screens, large amounts of treasure, etc. The French have smashed everything in a wanton way.'"

"What was the cause of this war?" asked Mr. Anson.

"It is a long story," said Dr. Hoddard; "but I will tell it to you in brief. In October, 1856, a Chinese vessel, the 'Arrow,' carrying the British flag, was boarded by Chinese officers. This was the cause of British hostilities against the Chinese. As for the French, a Roman Catholic missionary, M. Chapdelaine, had been murdered by Chinese in the province of Kwang-si. The United States had nothing to do with

WORSHIP OF ANCESTORS.

these troubles, and so refused to enter into an alliance against China. But to return to Gordon. I am glad you asked about him, for he is a rare Christian soldier and an earnest friend of missions. He was brought into such relations to the Chinese Government that, by his personal influence, he greatly aided in advancing the welfare of Chinese Christians; but, above all, he played so important a part in the putting down of the Tai Ping rebellion, that he became famous as a Christian soldier."

"What was the Tai Ping rebellion?" asked Bertie. "We heard of that when we were talking of pagodas, beneath the thirteen-storied pagoda of Tung-cho, and often friends have shown us 'traces of the work of the Tai Pings,' as they have said."

"Why do they call General Gordon 'Chinese Gordon?'" interrupted Bessie.

"I will answer both questions at once. They call Gordon, 'Chinese Gordon,' because of his part in putting down the Tai Ping rebellion, as the leader of the 'Ever-victorious Army,' a body of Chinese soldiers. The Tai Ping rebellion really had a very singular history. Once a peasant named Hung Siu-tseuen visited Canton, and heard a foreign Protestant missionary preaching in the streets. The tract distributor who was with the missionary gave the peasant a book of sermons by a Chinese convert, entitled 'Good Words for Exhorting the Age.' When he reached home. Hung looked through the volume and then laid it in his bookcase, to be forgotten for some few years. This was about 1833. Hung tried to get into a government office, but failed. After a few years the Opium War broke out, and Hung saw the wonderful fire-ships of the westerners. He became curious to learn about the religious views of these powerful western nations, and once more took down the little book. He had had some strange visions about six years before, and he thought he found the key to them in the little book; he had dreamed that a voice from heaven had summoned him to destroy all idols and to uproot idolatry. He and one of his first converts, named Fung Yun-san, became zealous preachers. An American Baptist missionary, Mr. I. J. Roberts, treated the converts with suspicion. But Hung went back and taught his converts how to baptize. The con-

THE STORY OF "CHINESE GORDON." 143

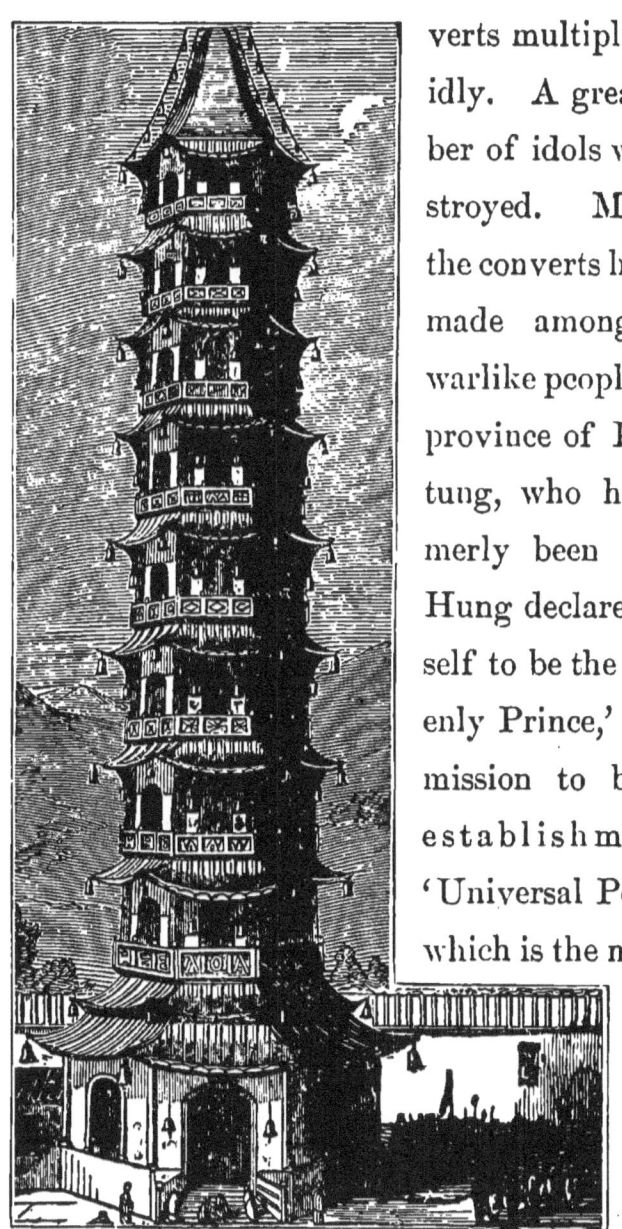

PORCELAIN PAGODA.

verts multiplied rapidly. A great number of idols were destroyed. Many of the converts had been made among some warlike people of the province of Kwangtung, who had formerly been pirates. Hung declared himself to be the 'Heavenly Prince,' and his mission to be the establishment of 'Universal Peace,'— which is the meaning of Tai Ping. The 'Heavenly

Army' rapidly increased in strength (just as the 'Salvation Army' has done in England and America), and when they finally gathered together to enter Nankin, where was the famous Porcelain Pagoda, Hung had an army of over ninety thousand followers. The Imperial Chinese troops sent to put down the rebellion were beaten in every battle. Before going into the fight, the followers of the Chinese Prophet-King knelt in the open field in prayer. They conquered city after city, and it seemed as if they must sweep the empire. They declared their belief in our Christian Bible, of which they had an imperfect translation in their own language. They observed the Lord's Day, and held religious services. They welcomed Europeans as 'brethren from across the sea,' and fellow-worshipers of 'Yesu.' We foreign missionaries tried to reach the Tai Ping leaders, and to teach them the truths of the Christian religion, but our efforts all failed."

"There was one thing I have heard of," said

Mr. Anson, "of which you have not spoken. The Tai Pings bitterly opposed the use of opium, did they not?"

"Yes, indeed," replied Dr. Hoddard. "They would not accept of the aid of a body of rebels, when attacking Nankin, because they would neither give up the use of opium, nor renounce idolatry. Possibly this may have had much to do with the fact that England loaned the aid of her soldiery to repress the rebellion, that she feared to lose China as a market for the opium that she raises in India. It was Gordon's business to obey orders, I suppose, and this may have been the reason for his taking the part he did in putting down the Tai Pings; but I think it more likely that the earnest Christian soldier saw that, while a few of the leaders were sincere in their intentions and in their devotion to Christ, the great mass were unchanged in heart, and were only after plunder and power. Probably it was to check their mad destruction of life and property, and to rescue the fair name of Christianity from the stains being put upon it, that Gordon consented to take command of the Chinese soldiery. In a letter that he wrote to his family March 24, 1863, he says: 'I have taken the step on consideration. I think that any one who contributes to putting down this rebellion fulfills a humane task, and I also think tends a great deal to open China to civilization.' . . . . 'I can say that if I had not accepted the command, I believe the force would have been broken up and the rebellion gone on in its misery for years. I trust this will not be the case. I think I am doing a good service.' He was now about thirty years of age. Armed only with a cane, Gordon led his soldiers into battle. He showed rare courage both in repressing mutiny among his own soldiers and in attacking the Tai Pings."

"Do you remember, papa," said Bertie, "when we were in Philadelphia, that we went to the room of the Baptist Historical Society, and that we saw a chest marked with the name of the missionary to whom Hung went for counsel? Mr. Lincoln told us that he thought that much information about the beginning of the Tai Ping rebellion might be found in the papers in that trunk."

"I wish that I could see those papers," said Dr. Hoddard.

"If my memory serves me, Mr. Lincoln said that the chest was left with the Historical Society on condition that it should not be opened for a certain number of years."

"To return to Gordon. When the war was over, the Chinese Governor Li offered Gordon a large sum of money above his regular pay. He declined it. He said in truth, 'I leave China as poor as when I entered it.' The British Minister wrote: 'Lieutenant Colonel Gordon well deserves Her Majesty's favor; for, independently of the skill and courage he has shown, his disinterestedness has elevated our national character in the eyes of the Chinese.' I have heard from many of the Chinese who served under Gordon in one way or another, that he was very pious."

"I remember seeing a picture of General Gordon standing with his finger on a map, and with some ragged boys about him," said Bertie. "When was it that he taught them?"

"Right after he left China," said Mr. Anson; "he spent all of his spare time and money in trying to help the ragged boys of London."

"Where did he go next? and where is he now?" asked Bertie, thoroughly interested.

"I supposed," Dr. Hoddard said, "that you had heard of his going to Upper Egypt; but then, of course, we who know a man, always follow his movements with interest; and, moreover, you were not born when Gordon was in China."

"Just now," said Mr. Anson, "he is the central figure in the events occurring in Egypt, and all England is talking of him."

"Yes, he went to Egypt," continued Dr. Hoddard; "and, later, to India and to South

Africa, and then, in 1880 he went to China again. Russia was threatening China with war, and the Chinese were disposed to fight the Russians. Gordon was sent for as adviser. I was standing by when Governor Li saw Gordon, and ran and fell on his neck and kissed him. Gordon counseled peace, and the Chinese Government accepted his advice."

"I suppose you know, Dr. Hoddard, that after his return to England, Gordon was planning to visit the Congo region, in West Africa. You will remember that the International Association, under Stanley, has been at work there, until, in 1884, when Stanley returned to Europe. There are some American Baptist mission stations on the Congo, and it could have been wished that Gordon had gone to that region. But he was ordered to South Africa. Later, he visited Palestine."

"Yes, and yet he was too active a man to go about 'globe-trotting,'" added Dr. Hoddard. "There was a man, a peasant, who, in the

Soudan, began a work wonderfully like the work of the Tai Ping leader in China. Egypt was in a precarious state, and the English had too much money invested in Egypt to refuse all needed aid of military forces. So it came about that Gordon was sent out again. In February of 1884, Gordon was once more in Egypt. What he has done since has hardly become a matter of history yet, for I know only what I have read in the uncertain newspaper reports. But Gordon seems to be succeeding in repressing the False Prophet, El Mahdi, of the Soudan. He never goes into battle without a prayer for the poor blacks against whom he fights. The slaves he captures he turns into loyal soldiers, giving them their freedom. His ideal is to see every slave in the Soudan set free. He has given to the missionaries of the Church of England every assistance in his power, in going to and from their mission-fields in Central Africa; and has contributed considerable sums of money to their mission work. As a Christian and a missionary, I thank God for raising up Charles George Gordon. His wonderful humility and marked disinterestedness, and remarkable fidelity and dauntless courage, have added lustre to his character as a Christian. We, in China, and they, of Egypt, can point with pride to Gordon as a specimen of the work of Christ's grace in a human soul."

The evening was well spent when the Anson family, led by Dr. Hoddard's servant, found their way back to their hotel. After several days of sight-seeing, they made preparations for their departure.

CHAPTER X.

HOUSEKEEPING IN CANTON.

OUR friends returned by junk to Tien-tsin, down the river, and thence to Shanghai by ocean steamer. At Shanghai they took a French steamer for Hong-Kong. Soon they were among the mountainous islands off the coast; and then, by a picturesque, narrow channel, entered the outer harbor, with the red, rocky hills of the mainland, and the high hills of Hong-Kong on the other. Then, with a sudden turn, the inner harbor was entered, and Hong-Kong lay before them.

"The city looked magnificent, suggesting Gibraltar; but far, far finer, its peak, eighteen hundred feet in height—a giant among the lesser peaks—rising abruptly from the sea above the great granite city which clusters upon its lower declivities, looking out from dense greenery and tropical gardens, and the deep shade of palms and bananas, the lines of many of its streets traced in foliage, all contrasting with the scorched, red soil and barren crags."

Great warehouses, cathedrals, colleges, and factories came rapidly into view. Over all waved the English flag; for the island belongs to Great Britain. Since Hong-Kong was so plainly a foreign city, and in scarcely any sense a Chinese city, the Ansons determined to move on to Canton. So, after a single night in the hotel at Hong-Kong, they took their places in a great deck-above-deck American river-steamboat, with three or four other European passengers, and some twelve hundred Chinese passengers. Canton lies about ninety miles up the Canton River from Hong-Kong, and the trip is through a level country, mainly covered with rice fields. To get to the wharf at Canton, it took nearly an hour's careful threading for the steamer to make its way among the boats of all sorts, house-boats, junks, and *sampans*, which filled the river. The boats of Canton are so numerous, that it seemed to Bertie as if fully half the people must live upon the water. The city lies on a level plain, and seems to be full of houses, all packed as closely together as sardines in a box. When the steamer reached the wharf, and while the Ansons were watching the crowds of Chinese as they went ashore, Mr. Anson felt some one touch him on the shoulder, and a cheery voice called out:

"Why, Mr. Anson, how do you do? How do you come to be on this side of the world?"

"My dear Dr. Balkom, how do you do? I did not expect to see you so soon. I thought that just as soon as we were settled I should hunt you up."

"But I got the start of you, you see. I saw your arrival mentioned in the Hong-Kong paper that came up during the night, and, while I was not positive, I felt almost sure that it was Anson, my old schoolmate, who had just come in on the French steamer."

Mr. Anson then presented Dr. Balkom to his family, and they prepared to go ashore.

"Just wait a moment, and I will get chairs for you. Mrs. Balkom will be expecting you and your family, and I will take you home right away."

"Why, doctor," interrupted Mr. Anson, "we are not expecting to quarter ourselves upon you."

"We will settle that by-and-by; but we will get home first, and do our talking there."

In a few moments Dr. Balkom returned with five bamboo chairs suspended from poles, and a couple of men to carry each chair. He spoke a few words in Chinese, and soon the procession wended its way through the narrow streets down by the river until the missionary quarter was reached. The face of Mrs. Balkom, smiling so pleasant a welcome as she met the friends of her husband at the door, seemed to them the most beautiful they had seen since leaving home —the gray hair lying smoothly on either side of the forehead, the calm, serene countenance, the patient, yet loving eyes—and her whole bearing seemed so mother-like to them, that it was a bit of home just to meet her. After a little pleasant conversation, Mr. Anson said:

"By the way, Dr. Balkom, what about my baggage? I have forgotten all about that."

"It will be here in a few moments. I left a trusty man to bring it home as soon as possible."

"But we must not quarter ourselves upon you. Indeed we cannot so far trespass upon your kindness."

"I assure you, to have my old classmate—yet he is not as old as I—is a privilege to both my wife and myself, and we cannot let you go. But let us be perfectly frank with each other. I suppose that you would like to stay in Canton several weeks at least, and yet you are afraid the care of your entertainment might be a burden to my wife."

"Yes, yes, that is just it," said Mr. Anson; "and we should feel badly if we added to the burdens that rest upon your good lady. I should greatly enjoy staying with you, but I know how busy all you missionaries are; and I know, too, the depth of the missionaries' purses, and my family is too large to thrust upon your hospitality."

"Well, if you think best—and I can appreciate your feelings—we shall have to give up our pleasant plan. Yet, not entirely, for I have a second string to my bow. One of our missionary ladies, Miss Sohn, who has just gone to America on a vacation, has a three-roomed bungalow right next to and adjoining our house. She left the key with us, and bade us make a free use of the house in her absence, if any guests should come. We can lend you bedding and crockery, and you will find everything else that is needed, in the house. I can hire for you a good cook, who understands some English; and Mrs. Anson can try her hand at housekeeping in China."

"Oh, that will be splendid," cried both Bertie and Bessie.

"Will this inconvenience you in the least?" asked Mr. Anson.

"No, not at all; and we shall be glad to have such good neighbors."

"It is kind in you to make the offer, and with Mrs. Anson's consent, we will accept it."

"Mrs. Anson can leave her housekeeping," added Mrs. Balkom, "entirely in Ah Ching's hands. She need only tell him how much money to spend—and I can help her in fixing upon the sum needed—and he will attend to the rest. My husband and I, and one of our native preachers, will be able between us to guide you in your sight-seeing."

The remainder of the morning was spent in unpacking trunks and in getting settled. Among the contents of the trunks were several very valuable volumes and some articles useful to a lady, which Mr. and Mrs. Anson had purchased in San Francisco for Dr. Balkom and his wife. These, Ah Ching took in next door, and said to Mrs. Anson:

"Lady, much obliged. She hardly speakee, but muchee cry."

After a hasty tiffin, or luncheon, Dr. Balkom

TEMPLE OF FIVE HUNDRED GODS.

came to take the Ansons upon their first round of sight-seeing. First of all, they went to see the Temple of the Five Hundred Gods. These are the Arhans, or pupils of Gautama Buddha. The temple is like all other Chinese temples, but it differs from all in the images of the deified disciples of Buddha. These are life-size, sitting on their heels, in Oriental fashion, each exhibiting the wonderful act for which he has been made a god. The eyes of one are always turned towards heaven, and are supposed never to have winked. Another held his hand above his head until it became immovable. Another has held his hand so steadily and softly that a bird has come and built its nest in it. Another became so holy that Buddha opened his disciple's breast and entered his heart. The idols are made of clay, and gilded over. Before each idol is a vessel of ashes for joss-sticks, and vases for flowers. The main altar, where prayers are offered to the whole five hundred gods, stands in the centre of the temple.

Dr. Balkom proved a very serviceable guide; for he had spent nearly twenty-five years in China,

HOUSEKEEPING IN CANTON.   161

and was thoroughly well acquainted with the people, and their language and customs. Bertie, who was at times a regular box of questions,

SALE OF PRAYERS.

found that Dr. Balkom could answer almost every question he asked. In reply to some of his questions, Dr. Balkom said:

L

"Canton—or, as the Chinese call it, Kwang-tung—has a population of about a million souls. Sixty thousand of these spend their lives, by day and night, upon the water. The city has a wall around it, about seven miles long; there are sixteen gates in the wall. Within the city are about one hundred and twenty temples. Most of the buildings are low."

"What are the high buildings that we saw as we came up the river?" asked Bertie.

"Do you mean the pagodas?"

"No; I have learned about those; but those great square buildings."

"Oh," said Dr. Balkom, "they are pawnbrokers' storehouses. The Cantonese pawn almost everything that they do not have in actual use, both to get money, and also to save the trouble of storage and the risk of thieves."

Just here they passed a temple, with a hall in front that was full of people.

"What are they buying?" asked Bessie.

"We will stop and see. These are all priests.

HOUSEKEEPING IN CANTON. 163

The two that you see at the desk by the wall are filling up blank prayers to suit the wishes of the buyers. They may be able to write, but the priests

BURNING PRAYERS.

persuade the people that they alone know how to write so that the gods will hear."

"Then do they read off these prayers? or do they make spit-balls of them, as they do in Japan?" asked Bertie.

"Neither," replied Dr. Balkom. "I will show you what they do with them; come this way."

He led the way through some small streets, until they came to a little temple standing in the midst of a clump of banana and palm trees. After waiting a moment, a bareheaded, barefooted Chinaman came to the keeper sitting by the door, and getting a light from him, touched it to a piece of paper upon which some Chinese characters were written, and held it until it was all burned up.

"That's the way the Chinese pray. They send up their prayers in smoke," said Dr. Balkom. "They send money, clothing, horses, etc., to their dead friends in the same way; that is, they make pictures of the money, or clothing, or horses, and burn them up. Most of those whom we saw buying prayers will take them either to the temples, where they will burn them before the idols, or they will take them home and burn them before the household altar. Here"—stooping and pointing to an object just within the door of the house they were passing—"is a household altar. Do you see that block of wood all carved, and with characters written upon it? That is an 'Ancestral Tablet.'"

The tablet to which Dr. Balkom pointed was made of wood, and was about twelve inches high and three inches wide. It consisted of three pieces, a pedestal, an upright piece, and a block upon which certain Chinese characters were carved.

"Often," said Dr. Balkom, "a place is cut in the back, in which pieces of paper containing the names of the ancestors are placed. Every day, incense and paper prayers are burned before this tablet."

"Do they pray to their dead fathers?" asked Mr. Anson.

"Yes, *to* them, not *for* them. They also go and pray at the graves of their ancestors. I

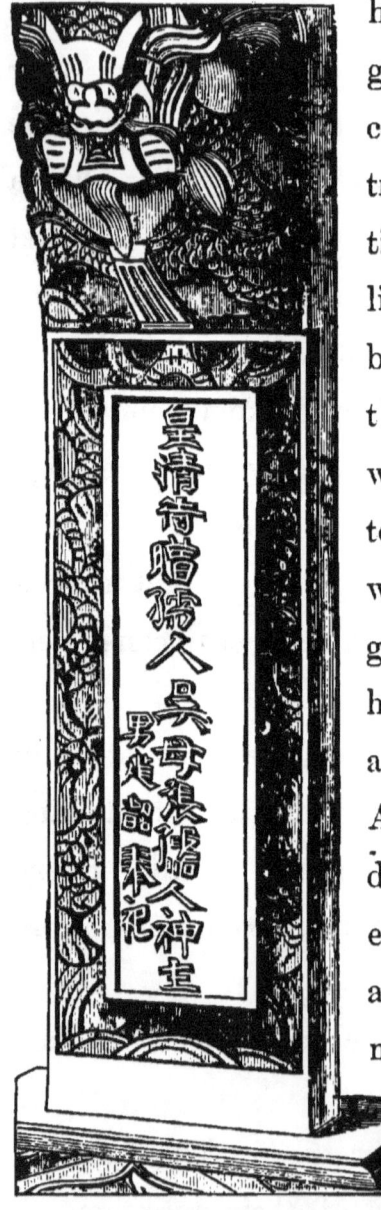

ANCESTRAL TABLET.

have at home a prayer, given me by one of my converts, which I will translate for you some time. The Chinese believe, you should remember, that every man has three souls: one of which at his death goes to heaven, one remains with the body in the grave, and one is brought home, and lives in the ancestral tablet. In April of each year, a day is selected, when especial worship is paid at the graves. Every man, woman, and child hastens away to the family tombs, taking offerings and candles to worship at the grave. To neglect this ceremony is counted a slight to one's dead parents."

This is the translation of the prayer offered at the grave which Dr. Balkom gave to Mr. Anson:

"TANKWANG, *12th Year, 3d Moon, 1st Day.*

"I, Lin Kwang, the second son of the third generation, presume to come before the grave of my ancestor, Lin Kung. Revolving years have brought again the season of spring. Cherishing sentiments of veneration, I look up and sweep your tomb. Prostrate, I pray that you will come and be present, and that you will grant to your posterity that they may be prosperous and illustrious. At this season of genial showers and gentle breezes, I desire to recompense the root of my existence, and exert myself sincerely. Always grant your safe protection. Most reverently, I present the five-fold sacrifice of a pig, a fowl, a duck, a goose, and a fish; also, an offering of five plates of fruit, with libations of spirituous liquors, earnestly entreating that you will come and view them. With the most attentive respect, this announcement is presented on high."

Dr. Balkom remarked, after reading and handing the prayer to Mr. Anson:

"To a Chinaman there is no greater sin than to neglect the worship of an ancestor; no greater calamity can happen than that he should die and be buried away from his native land. Almost every steamer that crosses the Pacific from America carries one or more preserved bodies of Chinamen, taking them home to be buried."

BRINGING HOME SOUL.

A few days later, when the Ansons, with the

native preacher, were sauntering in the suburbs, they met a man carrying a bamboo over his shoulder, from the end of which hung a ball with a coat below it. He was bringing home one of the souls of his dead father, which was to dwell in the Ancestral Tablet.

The weeks slipped away rapidly in the pleasant company of Dr. and Mrs. Balkom, and in ceaseless sight-seeing. The Ansons thought that, on the whole, the Chinese were not as lovable a race as the Japanese, but that they were fully as much in need of the gospel. During the latter part of their stay, Mr. Anson noticed a thoughtfulness on Bertie's face, whenever they began to talk about mission work in China. The noble character and self-denying zeal of Dr. Balkom so impressed the boy, that within his own heart there began to be started searching questions. It was pleasant enough to travel about as they were doing, but what if he were always to live in this noisy, filthy city of Canton? Why should he not become a missionary? There was evidently need of many more like Dr. Balkom. The questions were not to be answered at once. When the time came for saying good-bye, as the steamer was to bear them down to Hong-Kong, Bertie could not help feeling that there might be truth in Dr. Balkom's words:

"I feel, for some reason or other, that we may see you again in Canton, my boy."

In a day or two the Ansons were again upon the ocean, steaming around the corner of China, in the direction of the Land of the White Elephant.

CHAPTER XI.

IN THE LAND OF THE WHITE ELEPHANT.

IT had been Mr. Anson's purpose to visit Cochin China on his way to Siam, but the unsettled state of that country, on account of the French and Chinese wars, led him to propose going to Siam direct. So the family took a French steamer to Saigon, in Cochin China, and a sailing vessel from Saigon to Bangkok, Siam. This last was not so pleasant a way of traveling.

After crossing the bar at the mouth of the River Meinam, the Ansons took their places in a small tow-boat, and started up the river to Bangkok, thirty miles above the entrance. The banks of the river were lined with dense vegetation; gigantic palms and other tropical trees were covered with trailing vines coiling around their huge trunks. Here and there a fisherman's hut was built out over the river. Many small boats were plying to and fro. The party landed in, what seemed to them, the midst of a forest of cocoanut and other trees; but they soon found that it was the foreign portion of Bangkok. The native city was yet three miles further up the river. Mr. Anson had been informed, while in China, of the only foreign hotel in the city; and, under the guidance of the man in charge of the little steam-launch, proceeded to the place. The hotel was on the bank of the river, a little way above the landing; almost all of the houses front on the river, which is a sort of street for Bangkok. Very many canals run off from the river among the houses.

Bangkok is the Siamese capital, and has about half a million inhabitants; among these, there are more than twenty thousand priests of the Buddhist religion. There are multitudes of Chinese in Siam, as there are in all parts of the East, and they have their own temples and priests. It happened one morning, while Bertie was sitting on the veranda of the hotel, waiting for breakfast, that he saw a priest's begging-boat come down the river. After breakfast, he thought that it would be a good idea to write down what he had seen, as a part of one of his letters home.

"It is a curious sight to see the begging priests. They all wear yellow gowns, and their heads are so clean shaven that they look as if they had been polished. Each boat contains one priest and a boy-paddler. Before the priest stands a covered basket. The boy rows up before a house, then the priest, in absolute silence, takes off the lid of the basket; some one belonging to the house steps to the door, and takes from a kettle of rice a ladleful, and empties it into the priest's basket. The boy pulls away. Nobody speaks a word. The priests seem to be a lazy set of folks. They lie around smoking and chatting most of the day."

A day or two after, several missionaries came to see Mr. Anson, among them the venerable

Dr. Kean, who had been working among the Chinese, either in Siam or China, nearly fifty years. His long white beard swept his breast, and he seemed a veritable patriarch; yet the tenderly affectionate way in which he kissed Bessie, as he bade them welcome to Siam, won the hearts of all the Ansons. After a little pleasant conversation, he turned to Mr. Anson and suggested a stroll in the garden.

"I wanted to mention one little thing to you. I do not want to be officious, but as a Christian brother, I want to serve you, if I can. You can throw away my advice, or you can act upon it, as you like. My long experience in the East makes me see that which would escape the notice of another. If I am not mistaken, your good wife is beginning to be subject to that fever which is so great a trouble to foreigners in the East. She is but in the beginning of the attack. I do not think that you can check it while in these tropical countries. If I were you, I would say nothing to Mrs. Anson about the matter, but I would just quietly arrange my plans so that you shall see all that is of importance in Siam, Burmah, and India, and then hasten to the Holy Land, and thence to Turkey and home. You are here just in the best season, for the winter months are endurable in the tropics, or else I would urge you to retrace your journey directly to America, or to go to Europe."

"I am indeed grateful to you, Dr. Kean, for your thoughtful kindness. I assure you that I appreciate it. I have noticed a quietness, a depression of spirits, a loss of appetite and sleep, in Mrs. Anson, except when we were aboard ship. She then seems much better. I will reconsider my plans. This is, I suppose, one of the dangers to which we are subject in traveling. We shall try to see several temples in Bangkok, and in a day or two start for Rangoon, Burmah."

"The best temples for you to see, and they will give you an idea of all of the rest, are the Wat Chang Pagoda, and the Temple of the

Emerald Idol. I will be your guide this afternoon to Wat Chang, if it will suit you."

The same afternoon saw them in Dr. Kean's boat, ascending the river to the pagoda.

Passing through a large building with a sloping roof, our friends, under Dr. Kean's guidance, stood beneath the famous Wat Chang Pagoda. From one of the priests, Mr. Anson bought several handsome photographs of the pagoda and its spire. As he wrote in his journal on returning to the hotel:

"This is the most splendid temple I have seen since leaving Japan. The pagoda is shaped somewhat like a bell. It rises to a height, so Dr. Kean tells me, of two hundred and fifty feet. Every inch of its surface glitters with curious ornaments and carvings; the forms of men and beasts are like nothing in heaven above, nor earth beneath, nor waters under the earth. The spire is made of brick, and plastered on the outside. In large niches in the sides, about two-thirds of the way to the top, are

The Ansons.
WAT CHANG PAGODA.
Page 176.

images of Gautama Buddha, riding on white elephants made of shining porcelain, each facing one point of the compass. A sharp spire rises from the top. All over this temple tower, from the base to the summit, from every projecting point hang a great number of small, sweet-toned bells, swinging and ringing in the slightest breeze, filling the air with liquid melody. Within the Wat Chang enclosure, besides the pagoda and temple, are smaller temples, priests' dwellings, idols, a preaching-hall, and small parks, with flower and fruit-gardens, ponds, caves, and stone statues of famous saints, presenting a scene of bewildering richness."

"What are you thinking of, my boy?" kindly asked Dr. Kean, touching Bertie on the shoulder.

"I am trying to think of some verses that I recited at one of our school entertainments, about the bells. Those little bells swinging and ringing in the breeze, brought it to my mind. But all I can remember distinctly is this one verse:

> How they tinkle, tinkle, tinkle,
> While the stars that oversprinkle
> All the heavens, seem to twinkle
> With a crystalline delight;
> Keeping time, time, time,
> In a sort of Runic rhyme,
> To the tintinnabulation that so musically wells
> From the bells, bells, bells, bells,
>   Bells, bells—
> From the jingling and the tinkling of the bells.

"Yes, the bells above us do suggest that, and yet the poet's bells were bells that we never hear in this snowless land. They do jingle and tinkle melodiously. I often lie awake listening to them in the stillness of night. But shall we drop in and make a visit to his majesty, the White Elephant, while we are in his neighborhood."

"Yes," replied Mr. Anson, "we should like to see a genuine white elephant; we have heard so much about them in America lately."

"You must not expect to see a snowy-white

The Ansons. WORSHIPING THE WHITE ELEPHANT. Page 179.

elephant, but only a coffee-colored creature; I will warn you, to save you disappointment," added Dr. Kean.

"Do the Siamese actually worship the White Elephant?" asked Bertie.

"You will see for yourself. Here is his majesty."

On a splendid Persian carpet, stood a large yellowish-brown elephant. His tusks had golden rings upon them, and around his neck hung a huge necklace. Around the carpet's edge, a dozen Siamese were kneeling in prayer.

"Do they really believe that the elephant is a god?" questioned Bertie.

"Yes," said Dr. Kean. "They believe that Gautama Buddha lives in white elephants, and so the beasts are made sacred. This fellow was caught in the woods. The king and his followers received him with a great procession, and escorted him to his palace of a stable. Men were appointed as his slaves, and he was suffered to want for nothing. The Siamese regard the white elephant as the symbol of royalty. They stamp his image on their coins and embroider it on their flags. It is to them what the cross is to Christians, or the crescent to the Turks."

"That is why they call Siam the 'Land of the White Elephant,' is it?" asked Bertie.

"Yes; that is the origin of the name. Japan is the 'Land of the Rising Sun,' China the 'Middle Kingdom,' and so Siam is the 'Land of the White Elephant.' Now, I think you had better rest awhile, for to-morrow I want to take you to the Temple of the Emerald Idol. I must first go and get a Siamese friend to secure me the permission to take you in."

All through the night Mrs. Anson seemed restless and uneasy, though being able to secure some sleep. The next morning she seemed disinclined to go with the rest of the party. Mr. Anson's persuasions could not rouse her from her dejection. She insisted that the rest should go, and leave her alone. So Mr. Anson waited quite anxiously for Dr. Kean's coming, and his first greeting, as he met him in the walk to the hotel, was:

"Well, doctor, I am in a quandary. My wife passed a bad night, and she wants us to do our sight-seeing to-day without her."

"And leave her alone?"

"Yes, and leave her by herself."

"That will never do. It would do her more harm than good. But I will arrange it."

Then calling a servant, Dr. Kean dispatched him with a note to Mrs. Kean. After delaying their departure on various pretexts, finally Mrs. Kean put in an appearance. Without any delay she asked:

"Are you all going away to-day?"

"No; I am not going," said Mrs. Anson.

"Is that so? Well, I am almost glad, because I want you to myself to-day. We live away from the regular lines of travel, unlike our friends in India, or China, or Japan, and we rarely see travelers from our own lands. Dr.

Kean tells me that you are going to stay here but a day or two longer, and I am hungry to have you all to myself." And without giving Mrs. Anson an opportunity to say no, before she knew what she was doing, good, motherly Mrs. Kean had bundled her off to her boat, saying to the rest, "Don't be in a hurry to get back; I will take good care of mamma."

Soon Mrs. Anson was stretched out on a long bamboo chair, with Mrs. Kean at her side, knitting. In bright, cheerful conversation, an hour passed, and then one of Mrs. Kean's classes of Chinese women came to receive their usual daily instruction.

"Just sit right on the veranda here; we will have our lessons where the foreign lady can see us," she said to them, in Chinese.

Soon the strange sounds began to go to and fro among them. For awhile, Mrs. Anson studied their interested faces, but gradually the hum of the unintelligible sounds lulled her to sleep. After a refreshing nap, she awoke to find herself resting comfortably, while one of the Chinese girls was fanning her. Mrs. Kean soon returned with the news that luncheon was ready. The afternoon sped away so cheerfully that it seemed to Mrs. Anson as if the day was an oasis in a great desert of dullness and despondency.

Mr. Anson, the children, and Dr. Kean, were admitted without difficulty to the Emerald Idol's Temple. It proved to be one of the most remarkable and beautiful buildings of its kind in all the East. The outside was adorned with lofty eight-sided pillars, with queer doors and windows, all carved with a great variety of emblems, the lotus and palm occurring most frequently. This temple, like all Siamese temples, is built of brick, with roof after roof rising above it, and reaching out over great porches. The entire outside is plastered with a white cement. The roof is covered with differently colored tiles. But the altar was the most wonderful part of the temple.

During the afternoon, Mrs. Anson, in looking

over Mrs. Kean's books, found a volume containing the reminiscences of an English governess during her life in the Siamese Court. She happened to turn to the description of the Temple of the Emerald Idol, and wrote out, with Mrs. Kean's permission, her account of the altar:

"The altar is a wonder of dimensions and splendor—a pyramid one hundred feet high, terminating in a fine spire of gold, and surrounded on every side by idols, all curious and precious, from the bijou image in sapphire to the colossal statue in plate gold. A series of trophies these, gathered from the triumphs of Buddhism over the proudest forms of worship in the old pagan world. In the pillars that surround the temple, and the spires that taper far aloft, may be traced types and emblems borrowed from the Temple of the Sun at Baalbec, the proud fane of Diana at Ephesus, the shrines of the Delian Apollo; but the Brahminical symbols and interpretations prevail. Strange that it should be so with a sect that suffered by the slayings and the banishments of a ruthless persecution at the hands of their Brahmin fathers, for the cause of restoring the culture of that simple and pure philosophy which flourished before Pantheism.

"The floor is paved with diamond-shaped pieces of polished brass, which reflect the light of tall tapers that have burned on for more than a hundred years, so closely is the sacred fire watched. The floods of light and depths of shadow about the altar are extreme, and the effect overwhelming.

"The Emerald Idol is about twelve inches high, and eight in width. Into the virgin gold of which its hair and collar are composed, must have been stirred, while the metal was yet molten, crystals, topazes, sapphires, rubies, onyxes, amethysts, and diamonds—the stones crude, or rudely cut, and blended in such proportions as might enhance to the utmost imaginable limit the beauty and the cost of the adored effigy. The combination is as harmonious as it is splendid. No wonder it is commonly believed that Buddha himself alighted on the spot, in the form of a great emerald, and by a flash of lightning conjured the glittering edifice and altar, in an instant, from the earth, to be a house and a throne for him there!"

Within a few days the Ansons were once more upon the water, for the steamer was bearing them around the Malay Peninsula and up towards Burmah. Dr. and Mrs. Kean had accompanied them almost to the mouth of the river, and it was with great reluctance that they bade them good-bye. Often in Bertie's mind came up the cheerful, contented faces of their friends, and it was one more link in the chain of golden influences that was binding the boy's heart to the missionary work.

CHAPTER XII.

UNDER THE SHADOW OF SHWAY DAGON.

THE voyage to Burmah was an uneventful one. The Rangoon River, at its mouth about two miles broad, and with its shores low and wooded, narrows to about one-third of a mile in width opposite the great city of Rangoon. There are several hotels in Rangoon, and the Ansons had no difficulty in finding comfortable quarters. Most of the European houses are raised upon piles; they are built of teak boards, and have tile roofs. From the steamer's deck, the Ansons could see the English settlement, with several English-looking churches; and beyond, the large pagodas. Far away, to the horizon, stretched the forest of green palms, bamboos, and banana trees. The most wonderful sight in all Rangoon is the Shway Dagon, or Golden Pagoda. Indeed, this is the most monstrous pagoda, not only in Burmah, but in all the world. It is really a mile from the city, situated on a high hill. It so happened that the King of native Burmah had recently presented some diamonds, to be added to the "umbrella"—the *h'tee*—on the top of the pagoda; and the sloping sides were yet covered with the bamboo scaffolding used in re-erecting the *h'tee*. Consequently, no one of the Ansons had noticed the Shway Dagon until the day after their landing. Bertie, all impatient to see what was to be seen, had risen early, and, while glancing around, happened to see the gigantic pagoda casting its great shadow as the sun struck its sides. He ran in to his papa and begged him to come out and see the pagoda.

"Wait until I get my hat, and we will walk out to see it," said Mr. Anson. Bertie was all eagerness to go. After a brief stroll they reached the temple grounds and leisurely examined the great structure from without.

"There will be time enough by-and-by for us to examine it more thoroughly; besides this, we have not yet had breakfast. I imagine that we should have some difficulty to get about in the temple grounds, unless we had some one to guide us," Mr. Anson replied to Bertie's suggestion that they go inside.

While seated at breakfast, a servant brought in a card, with the name "Rev. I. K. Wilson and wife" upon it.

"I do not know who this can be," said Mr. Anson; "but, doubtless, it is some one of our kind missionary friends come to look us up. I will go right out to see them."

Advancing to the parlor, he met a dark-eyed young man, who held out to him his left hand—for his right was missing—saying:

"I presume that you do not know me, though I recollect you very well."

"No," replied Mr. Anson, "you have the advantage of me."

"I used to be one of your Sunday-school at

Dickson, Ohio. You had not then become a minister. May-be you will remember me as the little boy—I must have been about seven years old then—who used to bring grasshoppers and toads to Sunday-school. I do not know that you knew that I did it, for you never caught me at it; but I think it likely that you suspected me."

"Well, well, are you that little chap? And *you* a minister and a missionary! I never thought it then," added Mr. Anson.

"Yes, and I heard and remembered more of what you said, than you thought that I did. Well, now that you recognize me, I want you to come home with me. My wife and I are alone, and we would be real glad to have you occupy our spare room."

"No, I cannot do that"—and Mr. Anson told Mr. Wilson of his plan in this tour in Asia. "You missionaries are all warm-hearted and hospitable, but I am so confident that, with my entire family, I should be a burden upon you, that I have determined, wherever it was possible, to look out for myself."

"Well, I do not want to insist in pressing my home upon you, but you will, at least, bring your family and dine with us occasionally during your stay. I came to know that you were here by hearing one of our brethren speak of your visit to Japan; and from his description, I was quite sure that it was my old teacher of whom he was speaking, and so, with my wife, hastened in to be the first to claim you."

Just then the rest of the Ansons came in, and shortly Mrs. Anson and Mrs. Wilson were having a quiet chat together, while Mr. Anson proceeded to get Mr. Wilson's advice as to the best way to use the week that would elapse before a steamer would leave for Madras. Mr. Wilson suggested a day or two at Maulmain, and the rest of the time to be spent in and about Rangoon. Mr. Anson had already mentioned the state of Mrs. Anson's health.

"Suppose," suggested Mr. Wilson, "that to-morrow morning, just before sunrise, while it is yet cool, you and I and this young man climb to the top of Shway Dagon. You can get a glorious view from its top, and we can get up with no great difficulty."

"That will be like climbing up the Pyramids of Egypt, will it not?" inquired Bertie.

"Yes; very much like it," Mr. Wilson replied, adding, "you must not go into the sun without an umbrella, nor had you better go out of doors at all during the heat of the day. About four o'clock, when I have dismissed my teacher, I will come and take you through the grounds of Shway Dagon."

In the afternoon of the same day, the three strolled through the streets of Rangoon out to Shway Dagon. Something attracted Bertie's eyes, and he said: "What are those things for?"

"Those are griffins, or guardian dogs. They are put there to keep out evil spirits. I suppose that we shall not be troubled by them."

Passing between the griffins into a long passage-way, the Ansons found some very humble and yet very costly paintings—not very beautiful, but with so much gilding as to make them costly. "These show the tortures of wicked people," explained Mr. Wilson.

Then coming to the foot of a flight of stairs, which they climbed, they found themselves upon a platform, about a thousand feet square, and from the middle of the platform rose the great golden pagoda, some five hundred feet in diameter at the base, and towering to a height of three hundred feet.

"Do you think you will be afraid to climb up there, Bertie?" asked Mr. Anson.

"We shall hire a few coolies to help us; they will not let us fall," said Mr. Wilson.

For an hour they rambled about the platform and grounds, among the smaller pyramids. Within the pagoda are some shrines and idols; the larger idols being made of brick and mortar gilded over, and the smaller ones of metal.

"I will bring Dr. Finney, our veteran missionary father, to see you to-night," Mr. Wilson said. "He has been here some twenty-four or five years. He knows all about Burmah, and can tell you, as he told it to me, the story of the Shway Dagon. You will be interested in it, I know, and it will give you a better understanding of Buddhism and pagodas than you can get otherwise."

Mrs. Anson, looking pale and weak, met Bertie and his father on their return. Bessie had stayed to care for her mother in their absence. Mr. Anson's heart was full of anxiety as he noticed Mrs. Anson's appearance. He made no other remark, however, than to say:

"Dr. Finney and his wife are coming to see us to-night. I remember seeing Mrs. Finney some years ago, and I think that she will help you to feel quite bright and cheerful. Mrs. Wilson is coming for you with a pony and 'trap' to-morrow morning, when Mr. Wilson takes us to climb the Shway Dagon."

"What is a 'trap,' papa?" asked Bessie.

"Don't you remember the low, broad carriages that we saw in Yokohama and in Shanghai?" asked Bertie. "Those are 'traps.' Is Mr. Wilson rich, papa?"

"No; one of his friends, an English merchant, has bidden him use it whenever he wants, while he is taking a business trip up to Calcutta."

Dr. Finney was a quiet, gentle-voiced, yet evidently learned speaker. He had translated the Buddhist legends from the Burmese, and had made himself familiar with the whole history of the Shway Dagon. Bertie sat in a bamboo chair, a little outside of the circle gathered upon the veranda, and, in the dusk, jotted down a few catchwords, from which he wrote out afterwards, with his father's help,

THE STORY OF SHWAY DAGON.

"Two brothers from Burmah, once upon a time, made an offering to Gautama Buddha.

He, in return, gave them eight hairs that came out when he stroked his head. He told them to build a pagoda over them. They started to return home, but on the way lost six of the hairs. In a miraculous way, they found them again. A good spirit, a sort of fairy, told them where some other relics, of which Gautama had spoken, might be found. They dug a hole, and secured a water-scoop of one great saint, a robe of another, and the staff of a third. They built a shrine over these relics and the eight hairs. Others, later on, enlarged the pagoda over the relics, until it got to be of its present size. About four hundred and twenty-five years ago, a Burmese king cast a gigantic bell for the pagoda. The whole of the outside is covered with gold leaf, a little 'patchy,' because put on at different times, and with gold leaf of different fineness. The *h'tee*, or umbrella-shaped finial on the top, is made, as you will see to-morrow, if the guard will let you go near enough, of a number of gilded iron rings, from which hang a great many little silver and brass bells, that are swung and rung by the wind. Not long ago, one of the kings put up a new *h'tee*. It was studded with diamonds, and was said to be worth three

WORSHIPING A TOOTH OF BUDDHA.

hundred thousand dollars. The present king has given a few gems.

"The bell near the pagoda, big enough for a man to stand upright within it, was once carried off by the British. But they could not load it, it was so heavy, and it fell into the sea. The Burmese say that the gods restored it to the Shway Dagon. The bell has a great deal of gold in it."

After much pleasant conversation, the Finneys and their friends retired, leaving the Ansons alone. The next morning they were to rise early and make the ascent of the pagoda. But in the night a fierce wind blew, and so shattered the scaffolding that it was deemed unsafe for people to climb it.

The next morning, therefore, instead of going to Shway Dagon, together with Mr. Wilson, the Ansons went aboard the little steamer that was to bear them to Maulmain. As they entered the Salwen River, on which Maulmain is situated, Mr. Wilson pointed out the enclosure in which is the grave of the first Mrs. Judson; where sixty years ago her body had been laid away to rest.

Rangoon and its neighborhood was level and flat, but Maulmain was situated in a hilly country. Pagodas crown every hill-top. It seemed to Mr. Anson as if the whole neighborhood was full of historic associations with Dr. Judson's work. If Bertie had been impressed with his visit to the missionaries in Japan and China and Siam; if any feelings that possibly he ought to be a missionary had been started in his heart, by his conversations with Sasaki, or with Dr. Kean, he was much more moved by the sights of Maulmain, the missionaries' graves, their old homes, and the scenes of their labors. Here, for the first time, he ventured to tell his mamma of what he had been thinking. Pressing him to her heart with all a mother's love, she said:

"We should be glad to have you always within easy reach of us, Bertie. We love you

dearly. It would indeed be a great sacrifice"
—and the tears began to flow at the thought of
a separation—"to have you thousands of miles from father or mother. Yet you will be a man

PAGODA OF MAULMAIN.

then, and we must not let our love for you be stronger than our love for our Saviour. Do not make any promises, my boy; but think about it, pray about it, and our Heavenly Father will surely tell you what to do when the time comes."

"What is that, mamma?" Bertie had not yet, he felt, grown too old to use the childlike "mamma."

"Don't you recognize the bells, my son? They are the pagoda bells. On the Maulmain pagoda's *h'tees* the bells are almost all of silver. How sweetly the bells ring! Did you ever read Mrs. Emily Judson's poem, 'Watching,' the one that was composed while Dr. Judson lay in his sickness? No? Let me repeat a few of the lines:

> On the pagoda spire,
> The bells are swinging,
> Their little golden circlet in a flutter,
> With tales the wooing winds have dared to utter,
> Till all are ringing,
> As if a choir
> Of golden-nested birds, in heaven were singing;
> And with a lulling sound,
> The music *floats* around,
> And drops like balm into the drowsy ear;
> Commingling with the hum

> Of the Sepoy's distant drum,
> And lazy beetle ever droning near.
> Sounds, these of deepest silence born,
> Like night made visible by morn;
> So silent, that I sometimes start,
> To hear the throbbings of my heart,
> And watch, with shivering sense of pain,
> To see thy pale lids lift again.

For several long hours they conversed together of Dr. Judson's earnest career, and, when they knelt together, side by side, in silent prayer, Bertie felt that he had been brought to know more perfectly that his young heart and his whole future life belonged to his Saviour. An earnest prayer for God's guidance of their son went up from both father's and mother's heart, after Mrs. Anson had told her husband of their boy's thoughts.

"Perhaps," suggested Mr. Anson, "God will send him as my substitute." The tears trembled in his eyes, as he once more recalled his own desire to be a missionary and the denied pleasure. "God save my boy from such a disappointment as mine!" he said to Mrs. Anson. "We must try to train him physically, as well as mentally and spiritually, to qualify him for his work."

After a thorough exploration of the pagodas of Maulmain, and after another day of pleasant Lord's Day worship with the Christians of the city, the Ansons and Mr. Wilson started on their return to Rangoon. Mrs. Anson seemed, owing doubtless to the short trip from Rangoon to Maulmain, to be in somewhat better health than when they landed in Burmah.

The evening before they set sail for Madras, the missionaries of Rangoon met for their monthly missionary prayer-meeting. The piety and devotion of the missionaries was apparent in their prayers and words, and Mr. Anson seemed to feel that his own spiritual strength had been revived by being in the meeting.

"Yet," thought he, "how hard it must be where the missionaries are situated in lonely places, and where from year's beginning to year's end they hear no other voice in prayer than that of those who look to them for direction! Surely they need our prayers."

Nor did the memory of the missionaries, especially of Mr. Wilson and of Dr. Finney, fade away, as, from the steamer's deck, they waved their hands in a good-bye.

CHAPTER XIII.

FROM RANGOON TO MADRAS.

AS the wind blew steadily from the east, the vessel spread all its sails, and under press of steam and sail the passage from Rangoon to Madras, from Burmah to India, was quickly made. The Bay of Bengal is "the vast and wandering" grave of our great Dr. Judson; the Indian Ocean is the mighty tomb in which the precious remains of Dr. Binney are laid. Here their bodies rest, till the sea gives up its dead. Here, not far from the land they loved, whose graves shall yield their dead, too, when the Lord shall come.

Many boats were at the steamer's side almost as soon as she had anchored. The boats, as Bertie saw at once, were unlike any of those that they had seen in other countries. They were made of long planks *sewed* together. The seams were calked, yet appeared to be leaky. The flat bottom was covered with twigs, to keep the feet of the passengers dry. The sides seemed to be bent very easily, but in that consisted their safety. The oars, Bessie thought, looked like huge spoons. It was a delicate task, getting to shore without a wetting. The sea is always rough, the waves always rolling, and the surf always breaking. There is a huge harbor in process of building at present; gigantic breakwaters are to enclose a basin nearly a thousand yards square. Had the Ansons come a few years later, they might have been saved much unpleasantness in landing. As it was, Mrs. Anson and Bessie had to be let down into the little Masula boats in arm-chairs lowered by ropes. It seemed, sometimes, as if the tiny boats would be swamped by the waves. But the Ansons reached the beach in safety, and were carried through the wet sand by the boatmen.

Gharries, or bullock-carriages, stood along the beach, and Mr. Anson put Bessie and Mrs.

Anson into one, while he and Bertie trudged behind, screening themselves from the hot sun by their white umbrellas. They went immediately to the hotel nearest the landing, kept by a Swiss lady. The voyage had greatly strengthened Mrs. Anson, and, once more, her husband ventured to hope that they could complete their tour more leisurely, and take in all the places they had planned to visit. Mr. Anson had hoped to go by the railway, and visit Bangalore, Trichinopoly, and Madura, taking his family with him. Later he had thought to take a steamer and proceed to Calcutta. It was now midwinter; yet the heat at noonday was very oppressive, and Mrs. Anson seemed to feel almost immediately the change from the sea to the shore. This disconcerted Mr. Anson's plans, yet he knew not how to re-arrange them. As had happened everywhere else, so in Madras, the American missionaries began to call on Mr. Anson. It was one of the pleasantest parts of the journey, this privilege of meeting so many of the missionaries. Some of the missionaries were resident in Madras; yet others had come to attend a meeting of the missionary workers among the Telugu people. Among the rest were several who had just returned from a furlough in America, and had delayed their departure for Guntoor and Nellore, until after the missionary meeting. Mr. Anson met these friends at the gathering to which he had been invited. In the course of conversation, one of them, Mr. Newhold, from Guntoor, hearing Mr. Anson mention that his plans were upset and that he scarcely knew what to do, suggested a scheme, which Mr. Anson soon afterwards adopted. Mr. Newhold remarked:

"It will be better that Mrs. Anson should be as little exposed as possible to the dangers of a land residence. Yet you would wish her to see as much of the country and people as possible. The places which are of great missionary interest are right along the road to Guntoor, Ongole for instance. Now you and your family can leave Madras and go with me to Guntoor. I will see you across the Godavery River to Masulipatam, where the Calcutta steamers stop. Then you can all go on together to Calcutta, or Mrs. Anson and Bessie can take the steamer, and yourself and your son proceed overland by way of Juggernaut to Calcutta."

"But I think that I had better not leave Mrs. Anson; she is hardly able to look out for herself, in her condition of health," replied Mr. Anson.

"I notice," said Mr. Newhold, "that she looks as if the fever had touched her. But you can determine your course after you get to Guntoor. Yet, wait a moment, till I speak with one of the ladies yonder."

"Now, do not go to any trouble," called Mr. Anson after him.

Mr. Newhold approached the ladies, saying:

"May I interrupt you? I would like to ask if any of you ladies are going on to Calcutta shortly."

"Yes," said a rather stout, yet active and pleasant little woman. "I am going, but not at once. I must wait over a steamer till our Miss McCally comes back from Madura, where she has gone to see a friend."

"Let me see," continued Mr. Newhold; "that will be about three weeks from now, will it not, Miss Bristow?"

"Yes, just about."

"Could you look after a lady and her daughter, in Calcutta, if they met you on the steamer at Masulipatam? That is the lady over yonder."

"Well, I think that I could. Shall I have to look after her husband too?" she asked, with a smile.

"No, I think that he may go by land to Calcutta, while he sends his wife by sea."

"Of course, I shall be glad to do anything for her."

"And anybody else, Miss Bristow; you are wonderfully kind-hearted," appreciatively remarked Mrs. Newhold.

"Please introduce me to her, Mr. Newhold, and then I can tell her, myself, how glad I shall be of her company," said Miss Bristow.

The matter was soon arranged; and a day or

WORSHIP IN TEMPLE OF KRISHNA.

two afterward, in company with the Newholds and several other missionaries, the Ansons set off for Guntoor. The first ninety miles was traveled in a boat on the canal; the rest of the way to Nellore—about seventeen miles—by palanquin. At Nellore, they arrived just before the Lord's Day. It was a delightful day of rest, spent in worship with the Telugu Christians. Just about sunset ten or eleven candidates were baptized in the baptistery in the midst of the garden, a most beautiful spot for the burial ceremony, the resurrection ordinance.

While at Nellore, Dr. Downing showed to Mr. Anson a little gold coin that has a curious history. About a hundred years before, a peasant ploughed against some brick-work. On digging deeper, he found the ruins of an old Hindoo Temple of Krishna, or Juggernaut. The centre of this worship is now carried on farther up the coast. Many pictures of that worship, as it existed in olden times, are yet to be had. Underneath the temple, this peasant found a pot full of Roman coins and medals of the second century after Christ. They were sold as old gold and, all but thirty, were melted down. The one in Dr. Downing's possession had the name of Trajan upon it. It seemed strange to find old Roman coins in a Hindoo Temple.

Leaving Nellore, about seventy-five miles further on, they came to Ongole. Ongole is only about one-fourth the size of Nellore, but it is a town occupying a large place in the hearts of American Christians, because of the famous ingathering of thousands of Telugu converts in the church at this place. The pagoda of a heathen shrine towered up on one side, as our friends approached Ongole, while the missionary buildings gleamed in the sunshine on the other. In the background rose the hill upon which Dr. Jewett, in the days of discouragement, had prayed God to save Ongole, and God responded by sending Mr. Clough, the earnest and successful missionary.

Here, again, came impressions which strengthened and deepened the convictions in Bertie's heart. The hours flew by all too quickly during their two days' tour among the Christian hamlets. The visit to "prayer-meeting hill," the repetition of the story of the great occurrence on its top, the prayer-meeting that the visitors held there, were events never to be forgotten.

TEACHING A CHILD TO WORSHIP GANESHA.

Beyond Ongole, just before reaching Guntoor, in passing a shrine, Bessie, who had left her palanquin, peeped in. Running quickly to her mamma's palanquin, she motioned the bearers to stop, and then asked her mamma to come and see something. Walking to the entrance of the shrine, they saw a Hindoo mother, with her veil thrown back, kneeling, and holding her little boy's arms, while evidently teaching him to say his prayers to an ugly old idol with an elephant's head.

"What is it?" called back Mr. Newhold.

"Something very funny," said Bessie.

"Yes, and very sad," added Mrs. Anson.

"That is Ganesha, the God of Wisdom," said Mr. Newhold. "He is a very popular god. He is, as you see, partly a man and partly an elephant. The children in the schools are taught to pray to him, and he is adored by all who wish to become acquainted with Hindu learning and so-called wisdom. You will see his images and shrines in temples and schools, and also, occasionally, under the trees by the roadsides. I will show you one about a mile further on."

When they reached this wayside idol, Mr. Newhold stopped, and all rested in the shade before the great idol.

"What is the elephant's head for?" inquired Bertie.

"The elephant is one of the most sagacious of animals; the Hindus recognize this, and they choose to use the elephant as the symbol of wisdom and prudence and sagacity, as others worship the serpent as the symbol of cunning, and the sun as the symbol of power. Ganesh, or Ganesha, as we generally call him, has his great festivals, like the other gods. There is one festival, up in northern India, so I have read, where they place Ganesh upon a boat, and, accompanied with other boats containing priests and musicians, they row up and down the Ganges. The crowds that line the shore make the air to resound with their shouts and songs."

Passing Hindus stopped, even while the visitors tarried, and mumbled over prayers to Ganesha.

A WAYSIDE IDOL.

Guntoor was reached soon, and the party were

GUARDS BEFORE THE HINDU TEMPLE.

made quite at home in Mr. Newhold's quarters. On Mr. Newhold's suggestion that Guntoor was a remarkably healthy town, Mr. Anson concluded to stay here during the three days that must elapse before the steamer would leave for Masulipatam. There were no temples of any note in the vicinity of Guntoor. A single trip was made to the hills, a short distance back of the town, to visit the cave temples. Before the entrance of the chief temple stood a pair of mystic horses, with their grooms, the whole being the guardians of the place. These cave temples were at one time Buddhist places of worship; but long since they were converted into Hindu temples, and the images of Buddha altered into Hindu gods.

In the pleasant and cheerful home of Mr. and Mrs. Newhold, the days passed swiftly away. The little, one-storied bungalow, with its simple furniture, seemed a little paradise, owing to the warm hospitality, and the quiet yet sincere piety of the home-keepers. There were but few servants about.

"This is one reason," said Mrs. Newhold,

"why we prefer so small and slightly furnished a bungalow, that we need fewer servants. In India, a servant can do only one thing. If you see some dirt on the floor, and tell a chambermaid to brush it up, she cannot do it, but will tell the head-servant to send the sweeper to brush up the dirt. If you take a bath, you must have one servant to fill the tub and another to empty it. The more you multiply your conveniences, the more you must increase the number of servants."

Bessie was particularly delighted with one of the Hindu women, who, on becoming a Christian, took up her residence on the compound. She had learned a little of the English language, and seemed to take a great deal of pleasure in trying to talk with Bessie. Her expressions of Christian joy, and her delight in the Scriptures, touched the little American girl's heart.

Mr. Newhold accompanied the Ansons across the Godavery River, and saw them safe in Masulipatam. Before returning, he secured as a guide for Mr. Anson, an Eurasian, a man whose father was an Englishman, and whose mother was a Hindu. This Eurasian, John Christian by name, was to take the entire charge of Mr. Anson and Bertie, and to accompany them to Calcutta.

CHAPTER XIV.

JUGGERNAUT AND KALI.

THE British India Steam Navigation Company's steamer was very nearly on time at Masulipatam, and as the Ansons and Mr. Newhold reached the head of the gangway, they saw the bright, round face of Miss Bristow shining upon them.

"I am glad to see you once more. Are you better or worse than when we left you at Madras? I mean, do you feel stronger? We shall take good care of Mrs. Anson, when we get her in our Mission Home in Calcutta. I am planning to take her with me in some of my visits to the zenanas—where we met the Hindu women, you know. If she is quick at embroidery, we shall give her a chance to do some mission work, in trying to teach some of our Hindu pupils some new stitches."

"Won't that be splendid, mamma? I can help a little too; can't I?" asked Bessie.

"Yes, indeed," replied Miss Bristow; "we are glad to get all the help we can. I hope that Mr. Anson will not hurry to get to Calcutta, for we should like to keep you a long time to ourselves."

After a little, when Mr. Anson was walking the deck with Miss Bristow, he communicated to her his plans until reaching Calcutta.

"We are going to continue on the road running along the bay, through Ganjam, Puri—where the temples of Jagannath, or Juggernaut, are, and where we shall stay several days—and then by Katak and Midnapur to Calcutta. If Mrs. Anson should become ill, will you please send me word by special messenger to one of these places, and I will hurry on?"

"Certainly, if you wish it; but I hope that she will not need your presence," said Miss Bristow in assent.

"We shall not, but I shall rest more easy if

I know that, if I do not hear to the contrary, she is not ill. You are indeed wonderfully kind to us strangers. God bless you for it!" said Mr. Anson.

"We are expecting to 'entertain angels,' though not altogether 'unawares.' You may rest easy about Mrs. Anson, for we will give her the best care possible, should she need it. By the way, I have a letter which was brought to Madras just after you left, addressed in the care of one of your missionaries. He asked me to bring it to you when we should meet you here."

"Oh, this is for my son, and not for me. I received several letters from home, and I could not imagine from whom this could come. I will hand it to Bertie. Here, Bertie, is a letter for you."

"A Garfield five cent stamp! Then it is from America," said Bertie; "and from Philadelphia. I do not know that I am acquainted with any one there."

"Open it and see," suggested Mr. Anson.

Bertie did so and read:

"PHILADELPHIA, *Nov. 27, 1884.*

"MR. ALBERT A. ANSON.

"DEAR SIR:—You will pardon me, or I ought to say, *us*—for I am writing for others—for trespassing upon your good nature. Our teacher happened to see in one of the Chicago papers that your family were going around the world. She met your father at a Sunday-school Convention several years ago. We have a Mission Band, who are making a 'stay at home' tour in mission lands. We are reading and studying about the temples and the mission work in Asia. When we left China, we happened to hear of you, and our teacher suggested to us to write to you, so that the letter would reach you at Madras, and ask you to tell us something about the Juggernaut Temple at Puri. We will read your letter to our Band, and we shall be very glad to get information from one who has seen that of which he writes.

Our Band has made imaginary journeys in Japan and China, and are now in Burmah, and we shall reach India just about the time your letter reaches us. It is because we are so much interested in our plan of study—and we have such a good leader to help us in it—that we have asked this great favor of you.

"Yours truly,

"Eugene R. Copeland."

"Well, I think that I can do that much for them," thought Bertie.

Bidding good-bye to each other, the family separated, and soon the Masula boats bore Mr. Newhold, Mr. Anson, and Bertie ashore. John Christian met them as they landed, and took Mr. Anson and Bertie under his care forthwith. From Masulipatam to Puri the journey was uneventful. Many interesting temples and shrines were to be seen. But in Mr. Anson's mind, in spite of his efforts to the contrary, there was an uneasiness about Mrs. Anson until he reached Puri. When he came to that city, he sent John Christian to the collector's house—where the messenger was to have been sent—to see if any word had come from Miss Bristow. Finding none, he was considerably relieved, and went to examining, with interest, the Juggernaut temples. One afternoon, when somewhat wearied with sight-seeing, while his father lay stretched out under a *pankha,* or *punkah,* a swinging fan, Bertie began his letter to the young man in Philadelphia. In but a few days it would be Christmas time, and Christmas thoughts had been running through Bertie's head all day:

"PURI, *December 23, 1884.*

" MR. EUGENE R. COPELAND,

"DEAR SIR:—Your letter was brought to me just before we started for this place, where are the Juggernaut temples, of which you wrote. I write the answer under the shadow of the temples. Do not think that I found out all that I write, myself; my father and our Eurasian guide helped me in getting to know about the temple. We came here two days ago, and shall stay several days more.

"I think that your plan of study must be

TEMPLE OF JUGGERNAUT AT PURI.

a very interesting way of getting information, and better than just writing essays and reading pieces from missionary books.

"Papa suggests that I had better ask your indulgence before I begin, because my letter will have to be pretty long to tell you about the worship of Juggernaut and his temples. We have seen other temples and shrines belonging to his worship, but nothing so large as these at Puri.

"Juggernaut is a celebrated god. He is called the "Lord of the World." His images are as ugly as you can imagine. Generally, they are made of wood; in some temples placed three together, one of blue, one of white, and one of yellow. Juggernaut has many temples; the one at Puri, on the western shore of the Bay of Bengal, being the largest, and esteemed the most holy. The pagoda stands at the end of the principal street of the city, which is very wide, and lined with dwellings for the priests, small shrines, and other sacred buildings. The wall that surrounds the temple is twenty-one feet high, and forms an enclosure six hundred and fifty feet each side. The principal building rises to the height of one hundred and eighty-four feet. The main gateway is crowded with Fakirs, or devotees — 'cranks,' we should call them. On each side of the entrance is a mammoth lion. Just before us, as we enter, is an image of the monkey-god, Hanuman.

"The temple is dedicated to Krishna, or Juggernaut — sometimes written Jagan-nath — and his companions, Siva and Sathadra. The idols of each are rude, hideous looking sculptured blocks of wood, each about six feet high. The faces of these idols are hideous. Krishna is painted dark blue, Siva white, and Sathadra yellow. Before the altar an image of the hawk-god, Garounda, is placed. Every day, we are told, the idols are feasted. Their food consists of four hundred and ten pounds of rice, two hundred and twenty-five pounds of flour, three hundred and fifty pounds of butter, one hundred and sixty-seven pounds of treacle, sixty-five pounds of vegetables, one hundred and eighty-six pounds of milk, twenty-four pounds of spices, thirty-four pounds of salt, and forty-one pounds of oil. While the food is being placed before the gods, all but a favored few are excluded from the temple, and the doors are shut. There are over twenty thousand holy men connected with this temple, and we can easily guess that *they* help the idols to get rid of this great mass of food; at any rate it all speedily disappears. The idols, strange as it may seem, are washed and dressed daily with great seriousness.

"On June 18, Juggernaut's great festival occurs. Formerly, great multitudes assembled at this time from every part of the land. Men, women, and children, in crowds, thronged to the city days in advance, and waited with impatience for the festival day to come. The Car Festival, celebrated at Puri, is usually attended by more than five hundred thousand pilgrims, nearly half of whom are females. There is great suffering among these pilgrims, and many of them die of excessive fatigue, exposure to the annual rains, and the want of suitable and sufficient food. The plains, in many places, are literally whitened with their bones, while dogs and vultures are continually devouring the bodies of the dead.

"At the appointed time, each idol was washed, dressed in silk and gold, and placed upon his triumphal car. The car of Juggernaut consists of an elevated platform, thirty-four feet square, supported by sixteen wheels, each of them six and a half feet in diameter. It is covered with cloth of gold and costly stuffs, and a Juggernaut is placed under a canopy. Six ropes or cables, three hundred feet in length, are attached to the car, by means of which the people draw it from place to place. The whole car is covered with sculptures in the Hindu style.

"Thousands seize these ropes, as many as could get hold. In their fanatical frenzy, they crowded and shouldered and shoved one another, counting themselves happy if they could only lay a hand on the ropes. The Car Festival talking was heard outside the door, and in a moment John Christian pushed his way in, saying:

"Master, here is some one who wants to see you."

"Well, I will come right away."

Clad in his *pajamas*, Mr. Anson went to the door and found a stout, swarthy Hindu unwrapping a letter, which he handed, with many salams, to Mr. Anson.

"Mem sahib, the missis, she sick," he muttered to John Christian.

It was indeed true; Miss Bristow had hastily written that Mrs. Anson was taken sick. It might be only a slight attack of the fever, or it might be more serious. She had felt it her duty, as she had promised, to write Mr. Anson. They had good physicians, and everything would be done for Mrs. Anson that could be done. This only partially relieved Mr. Anson's anxiety. When he had dismissed the messenger, having paid him, he sat down to think it all over and to pray for the safety of his loved wife. He had not noticed John Christian sitting on the floor near the door. Finally, John ventured to say:

"Master, may I speak?"

"Yes, what is it, John?"

"A steamer will leave for Calcutta to-morrow. If master will go in it, he can be in Calcutta in two or three days from now."

"Can we? I am glad you have spoken of it. We will go."

"But, master, it is hard to get to the steamer, the surf is so very bad."

"Well, we will venture it."

"We might get some life-belts, master, and then it would be safer."

"Well, get two, John, for Bertie and me. You can go back to Guntoor, though I will pay you just as if you had gone on to Calcutta, for you have taken good care of us."

It was well that life-belts had been provided, for Bertie lost his hold when the boat rose on an unusually heavy wave, and was tossed into the water. For a moment, he struggled, and then allowed himself to be borne up by his belt. The boatmen soon fished him into the boat, though with considerable difficulty. The steamer was reached a few moments later, and Bertie soon appeared in a borrowed suit, while his own clothes were spread in the sun to dry.

When Calcutta was reached, Mr. Anson and Bertie entered one of the great crowd of *gharries* that stood about the wharf, and were quickly brought to the Woman's Mission Home. To his great joy, Mr. Anson found Mrs. Anson in an improved condition and able to sit up. In a few days she was able to drive out. Pleasant hours were spent in the Botanical Gardens, and in riding on the Maidan, or the Esplanade of Calcutta. From one of the missionaries' libraries, Miss Bristow had borrowed for Mrs. Anson's use, quite a number of illustrated volumes on India and its temples. In this way, Mrs. Anson sought to get that informa-

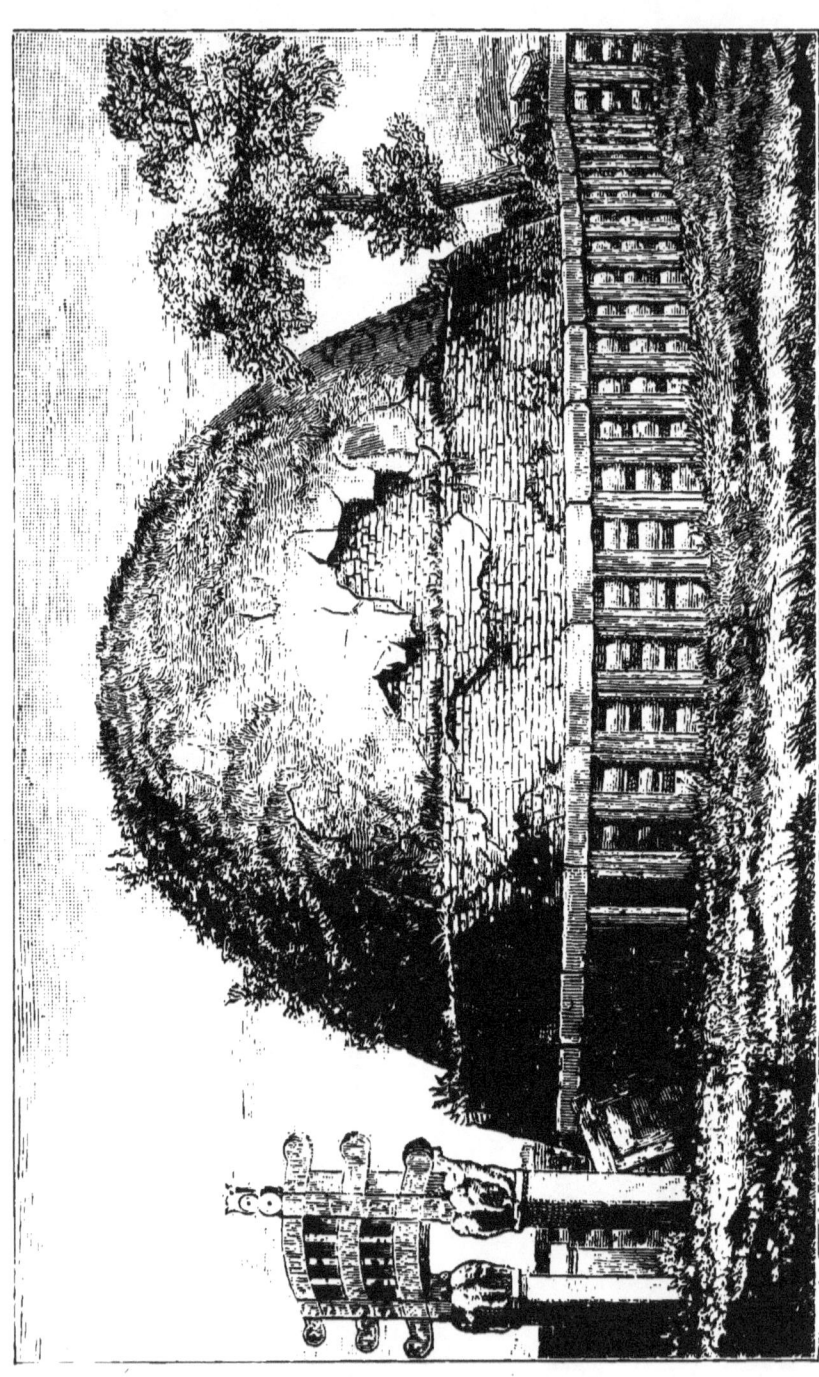

THE SANCHI TOPE.

tion which Mr. Anson was getting by actual observation. Her recollection of the pagodas of Rangoon and Maulmain caused Mrs. Anson to feel a particular interest in the Buddhist monuments of India, the land where the Buddhist religion was born. The great *topes*, or pagodas, as they might be called elsewhere, are all in ruins, yet they give signs of a former magnificence. One of the greatest of these is the Sanchi Tope. This is a dome-like structure of solid brick and stone, about sixty feet high. There are entrances at all the four points of the compass. These gate-ways are picturesque objects, even in their ruins. In the very heart of the *tope* an Englishman found small caskets, carved in precious marbles, containing pieces of burnt bone and ashes, all that was left of Buddhist saints who lived twenty-one hundred years ago. All the *topes* are monuments over Buddhist relics.

One hideous idol, which Bertie and his papa were taken to see, was that of the bloody goddess

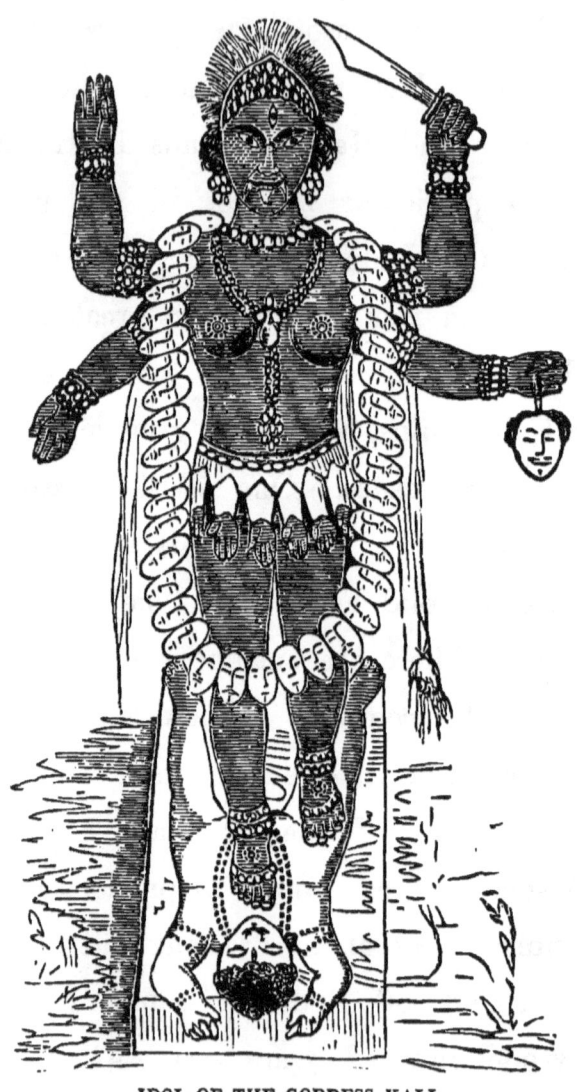

IDOL OF THE GODDESS KALI.

Kali. The missionaries persuaded, with little effort, Mrs. Anson and Bessie to refrain from going to Kali's Temple.

"This is a queer idol," said Bertie, to the missionary who had accompanied them to the temple. "I should think nobody would ever care to worship such a hideous, murderous-looking goddess."

"On the contrary, Kali is a very popular goddess, even though her images are the pictures of terror. She wears a head-dress of snakes, and a necklace consisting of a chain of skulls. In her hand she holds a murderous-looking knife. Kali is the wife of Siva, the destroyer. In September, a festival is held in her honor, called the Doorga-pooja. In all of Kali's temples, her idols are gayly adorned with flowers, and prayers are offered to her during days of dancing and singing.

There used to be a sect of murderous stranglers, known as Thugs, who were especially devoted to the worship of Kali, and who performed their murderous work as a religious service to that goddess. The story of this people opens up a chapter of the greatest cruelty, going far beyond all the ordinary records of crime. Yet it was all done from a religious motive, as well as for love of plunder. Strange that it could be so! The legend that accounts for their origin is as follows:

"A long while ago a giant demon infested this world, destroying mankind. The goddess Kali, to save mankind from utter destruction, attacked this demon and cut him down; but from the drops of blood that fell to the ground, immediately there sprang up other demons—a host of them. The Kali created two men, to whom she gave handkerchiefs, and whom she taught to strangle the demons without shedding blood. This was done, lest, if their blood be shed, more demons should spring up. Kali intended, in this way, to destroy the whole brood. When these men had strangled all the demons, she bade them strangle men in the same way, to repay her for her service to mankind. From these two men the Thugs came."

During all the time the missionary was giving this description of Kali and the Thugs, the people were coming and going, bringing their offerings and presenting their prayers. The conception seemed so horrible that it was a relief to get into the open air. Though, for many days, Kali haunted Bertie like a nightmare.

The health of Mrs. Anson improving, and the doctor interposing no objection, preparations for continuing the journey were made, and the overland trip was begun after several weeks had been spent in Calcutta.

CHAPTER XV.

OVERLAND THROUGH INDIA.

AN extensive railway journey in the land of elephants' *howdahs,* of bullock-*gharries,* of palanquins, of *masula* boats, was indeed a novelty. Since leaving Japan's short railroads, none had been encountered until now. There happened to be no one else in the compartment of the car that the Ansons occupied. The cars were unlike those in America, in that each car was divided up into rooms. Very soon after starting, Bertie found that there was a sort of shelf, or berth, that could be lowered over the wide, cushioned seats on either side of the compartment. They had started in the evening, by Miss Bristow's advice, so that Mrs. Anson might not become over-wearied. So the discovery of the bunks was quite opportune. Anticipating that the cold would be greater in traveling at night, Mr. Anson had provided four thick traveling rugs. He and Bertie mounted to the upper berths, and Mrs. Anson and Bessie slept on the sofas. For several hours they kept up a conversation, but late in the evening they slept quietly. They took their breakfast at Mokamah, where there was a delay of an hour or so. At Dinapur there was another opportunity of getting refreshments. The country along the railroad was low and flat, with mud-huts rising here and there. Everywhere the natives were getting ready their breakfast of plain boiled rice, the one great article of food in Asia. Often the railroad wound along the banks of the Ganges River. Many strangely shaped boats were moving to and fro. Occasionally, a crocodile could be seen, on the outlook for his morning meal.

Benares, the Holy City of India, was to be the first stopping point. At Mogul Serai, where they changed cars, Mr. Anson sent a dispatch —as he had been advised to do—to secure two rooms in the best hotel of Benares, and that a carriage might meet them. Thus they experienced no difficulty in getting through the crowd of porters thronging the neighborhood of the station. They crossed the river on the bridge of boats, and soon the carriage was climbing the cliff upon which Benares is built. The Ghats, or flights of steps, leading up to the temples, or sacred rest-houses for pious pilgrims, rose from the river's edge to the cliff above.

That same afternoon, under the guidance of a servant from the hotel, the Ansons took a ride upon the River Ganges in a steam-launch. This gave the best opportunity for a first view of the city, and also afforded many chances of seeing the scenes characteristic of the Holy City and the Sacred River. On the way they visited the Durga Temple, often called the Monkey Temple, because of the myriads of monkeys that live in the gigantic trees near it.

The steam-launch ascended the river to the

bridge of boats, and then, returning, stopped at the will of the passengers, giving them the privilege of climbing the Ghats and viewing the temples. From sunrise, daily, thousands of pilgrims come to bathe in the Ganges. The dying are brought there, and have their mouths stopped with the sacred

PRAYING BY THE RIVER GANGES.

mud. Their dead bodies are burned by the side of the river, and their ashes flung into its current. Here the faithful come to pray. The crocodiles occasionally catch some unwary bather and devour him.

Benares seemed to be, as Bertie quoted it from his Testament, "a city wholly given to idolatry." Devotees, pilgrims, and priests thronged the city. Temples were far more numerous than in any other city that they had seen, and it was easier to find an idol than a man, as was said of Athens of old time. Everywhere, the people made way to let the foreigners pass, not—as Bertie at first supposed—out of respect, but to avoid pollution.

"Where are we going next?" asked Bertie.

"We shall stop at Lucknow and Cawnpore, where we shall see the scenes of the great Sepoy mutiny; then we shall go on to Agra, and visit the great mausoleum, the beautiful monument to a loved wife, the Taj Mahal."

"What is the Taj Mahal?" asked Mrs. Anson.

"It is the sort of monument I should like to build, to show the world the depth of a husband's love for his wife. It is a beautiful building of marble, not very large, but wonderfully well built. I will tell you the story:

"A Mohammedan ruler of India, Shah Jehan, was married in 1615 to Princess Mumtaz-i-Mahal. She died in 1629. The Mogul determined to build the most magnificent monument that man could conceive of. For twenty-two years, twenty thousand workmen were engaged in erecting the building. It cost more than fifteen millions of dollars to build it. It has been called the jewel of India. An American traveler wrote, as I noted it in a fly-leaf in my guide-book here: 'As you approach it, it is not exposed abruptly to view, but is surrounded by a garden. You enter under a lofty gateway, and before you is an avenue of cypresses, a third of a mile long, whose dark foliage is a setting for a form of dazzling whiteness at the end. That is the TAJ. It stands, not on the level of your eye, but on a double terrace; the first, of red sandstone, twenty feet high, and one thousand feet broad, at the extremities of which stand two mosques, of the same dark stone, facing each other. Midway between, rises the second terrace, of marble, fifteen feet high, and three hundred feet square, on the corners of which stand four marble minarets. In the centre of all, thus "reared in air," stands the TAJ. It is built of marble—no other material than this, of pure and stainless white, was fit for a purpose so sacred. It is one hundred and fifty feet square— or, rather, it is eight-sided, since the corners are truncated—and surmounted by a dome, which rises nearly two hundred feet above the pavement below.'

"But we shall see it for ourselves, and we are losing some of this pretty scenery through which we are passing."

After a few days at each of the places of which Mr. Anson had spoken, and when their fondest expectations had been far surpassed, they continued on their journey to Delhi. The Ansons, when they reached Delhi, took rooms at the Northbrooke Hotel, kept by a European. All of the country hereabouts is full of interesting objects connected with the occupation of India by the English. Mr. Anson felt that, in the uncertainty of Mrs. Anson's health, it would be better to devote their attention chiefly to the temples and mission work of the cities where they stopped, and to give but a passing glance at historic sites.

"What is that great building yonder?" asked Bertie, one morning, as they passed out of the Chandni-Chowk, the bazar street of Delhi.

"It looks like a temple, yet it is unlike a Hindu temple in its style," answered his father.

"We will go near to it and find out." Looking through an opera-glass, Mr. Anson could make out certain strange characters carved on the sides of the entrance. "I do not know what that is; these are not Hindu letters."

"Let me see, if you please, papa," asked Bertie.

"Certainly, my son; but I think that you cannot read them either."

Bertie looked through the glass at them, and after a moment's thought, said:

250   THE ANSONS IN ASIATIC TEMPLES.

"I remember seeing something like them in your 'Arabian Nights Entertainment,' papa."

"Let me see again, my son. Yes, you are

GRAND MOSQUE OF DELHI.

right; they are Mohammedan letters. This must be a Mohammedan Mosque. We had better go back to the hotel and get a guide."

It was the Jam'i Masjid, the Great Mosque,

one of the finest in all India, before which they had been standing. With the guide they returned and climbed up the forty steps—as Bertie counted them—that led to the magnificent gateway. The gates were overlaid with plates of brass. Passing through the gateway, they stood within a court about three hundred feet square. In the centre is a marble fountain and basin. Climbing to the top of one of the minarets with the guide, Bertie looked down upon the rest from the dizzy height, and had a most extensive view of Delhi and all the surrounding country. When he returned, one of the Moslem priests took them through the mosque. After a little talk with the guide, the priest took them to one side, and slowly and reverently unlocked the door of a little closet cut into the solid marble. He opened a casket with great care, and showed to the visitors—*a single hair from Mohammed's beard.* To see only a hair sadly disappointed Bertie. All the show of mystery and caution had led him to expect some great thing.

"Pshaw! only a hair! Who knows if it is really Mohammed's?" he exclaimed.

"This astonishes me," said Mr. Anson to his wife, "that these Mohammedans should indulge in relic-worship, when Mohammed was so fierce a hater of idols and relics."

The building is of marble and red sandstone.

On another day, an excursion was made to the gigantic Kuttub Minar, a sort of tower or spire rising right out of the ground to a height of two hundred and forty feet. Standing in the midst of a vast plain, it seems much higher. It is about one hundred and forty feet in circumference at the base, and about twenty-seven feet at the top. Bands of inscriptions are carved in its sides of red sandstone, and it is, in all respects, a beautiful minaret. Its use, like that of all other minarets, probably, was for the Moslem priests to call the people to prayer.

From Delhi, the Ansons proceeded to Allahabad, and thence, without any delay, to Bombay. Just such scenes as one may see in cross-

THE FAKIR OF THE LONG HAIR.

ing the Alleghany Mountains, in Pennsylvania, were to be seen from the car windows, after leaving Jubbulpur, where a change of cars had been made. Notwithstanding the beautiful and romantic scenery, it was a pleasure to be settled in the hotel at Bombay. In a week or ten days the Ansons would bid farewell to India, and these last days must be crowded with sight-seeing.

Bombay was a city of temples. Holy men of all sorts seemed to abound. One order of priests, so Bertie learned, seemed bent on trying to see how many curious ways of self-torture they could devise. These were the Fakirs. One Fakir had a huge iron collar forged about his neck; another, whose long hair, as Bertie suggested, would furnish a safe hiding-place for the pestiferous insect that the man seemed to be trying to find as the Ansons passed him, had iron bands on his arms and ankles; another had held his arms immovably fixed above his head, while pious (?) people fed him.

256 THE ANSONS IN ASIATIC TEMPLES.

These men hope in this way to obtain favor with the gods, and the people rather respect and fear them, on account of their supposed

DYING BRAHMIN AND SACRED COW.

holiness. Truly in Indian minds, "cleanliness is" not "akin to godliness."

"Why, mamma, look at that man and the others standing around him. See, they are trying to keep his hand on the cow's tail," said Bessie, as they stepped within a temple, in the very heart of Bombay.

"He must be dying," said Mr. Anson; "he looks like it."

"Do they think that taking hold of the cow's tail will make him well?" asked Bertie.

"I do not know. We shall have to ask somebody to tell us. I wonder if any of these men can speak English. A great many of the Hindus of Bombay can, I know. I will ask that one standing alone." Then Mr. Anson drew near a poorly-clad, but intelligent looking Hindu.

"Do you speak English?"

"Yes, master, a leetle. I go Christian school sometime. I merchant's errand-boy."

"Can you tell me what that means?"— pointing to the sick man and the cow.

"Yes, he sick man; he Brahmin, high caste
R

man. He dying. That cow, holy cow. He keep hold of cow tail, will take him into— what you say?——" and he pointed upward.

"Heaven?' added Mr. Anson.

"Yes, heaven. I no believe that."

"No, no," said Mr. Anson; "you believe in Jesus Christ; you try to please him; then you go to heaven. I thank you for telling me what that means," as he slipped some pice —the Indian coin—into the man's hand.

On rejoining the group he explained it all to them.

"Isn't it pitiable! such superstition!" remarked Mrs. Anson; "and they might know better, if they would but listen to the missionaries."

"Well, good-bye, India!" exclaimed Bertie, as, a day later, the steamer bore them out of the harbor.

"God bring you light!" said Mr. Anson.

It was a bright moonlight evening, and, as

if in confirmation of his wish, he saw a sight in the sky, whither his eye had been turned. The floating clouds had seemingly massed themselves until they had assumed the shape of India, the edge clearly marked all the way from Arabia around by Ceylon, and up to Bengal, and then rounding again down to Burmah. As he looked, the edge alone was marked with a line of light. It seemed like a saying, "So is India lighted, but upon its edge, as it were." Just then, the full moon sailed out from behind the clouds, and threw its radiance full on the face of the cloud, and lo, India was bright with light, like all the rest of the clouds.

"So may it be! so shall it be!" thought Mr. Anson. That vision he never forgot.

CHAPTER XVI.

IN MOSLEM LANDS.

THERE were so many English passengers on the steamer who were going home, that a little tinge of home-longing touched the hearts of the other passengers. The voyage was a very quiet one. The heat was intense, so that the passengers spent most of the days and nights on deck; it seemed to be getting yet more uncomfortable as they approached the coast of Arabia and the entrance to the Red Sea. Aden is about ninety miles from the Straits of Bab-el Mandeb, the beginning of the Red Sea. When the vessel cast her anchor, scores of little boats, each with one or two Somali boys, paddled about the ship, crying, "Overboard! overboard!"

"What do they mean, papa?" asked Bertie.

"I do not know; let us wait and see."

Just then an Englishman flung a small coin

into the water; immediately each boat lost one boy, as they dived into the water after the money. At this moment, a fellow passenger said:

"The captain has posted the notice of sailing."

At once, most of the passengers turned to the stairway leading to the dining-hall, and then got themselves in readiness to go ashore, to escape from the heat aboard ship, and from the dust stirred up while the steamer took in coal. They found Aden to be the Gibraltar of Asia. Water is sold in Aden, because it is so precious; for there are no wells, or springs, or rivers.

Leaving Aden, and entering the straits, the steamer was upon the Red Sea. It seemed to Bertie that they were entering upon a sacred part of the earth.

"Why do they call this the *Red* Sea?" asked Bessie. "The water is not red."

"No," said Mr. Anson; "but the hills around are red, and the weeds yonder are red."

If it was hot in India, it was hotter on the Indian Ocean, and hottest on the Red Sea. To Mrs. Anson, the heat was so oppressive that it seemed as if she must die. The strong wind that blew from the south was almost scorching. But when about one-third the way through the Red Sea, they met the fresh breeze from the north, which is usually blowing strongly, and it greatly revived all the weak passengers. At the first, the thermometer in the cabin was up to 100°, but the third day it became so cool that the passengers shivered in their overcoats.

In passing Jeddah, the port of Mecca, Mr. Anson took occasion to tell the story of Mohammed, the Arabian camel-driver, who founded a great religion. Mohammedanism overran India, though it has since almost entirely lost its power in that country; it conquered, also, Arabia, Northern Africa, including Egypt; and crossed into Spain, where the Moors were finally conquered by the Spanish Christians; and it overran Turkey.

"In Mecca, Mohammed's birthplace," continued Mr. Anson, "is the 'Caaba,' or shrine, with the famous 'Black Stone,' which the Moslems, or Mohammedans, or Mussulmans, as they are variously called, believe to have been brought from heaven by angels. Mecca is seventy miles from Jeddah, and thousands of Moslems make pilgrimages to Mecca every year."

"Can we go there?" asked Bertie.

"No, indeed; any foreigner caught entering the city would certainly be stoned to death."

In entering the Gulf of Suez, one arm of the Red Sea, Mr. Anson pointed out to his family Mt. Sinai. Through the captain's glass, they could see but few signs of vegetation, and it seemed, indeed, a "wilderness."

"Now we shall soon cross over the spot— though no one knows to a certainty just where it is—where the Children of Israel, under Moses, crossed the Red Sea," said Mr. Anson.

A few hours later, the steamer cast anchor some distance from the shore, just opposite Suez.

Suez is a decayed-looking, ruinous town, having about fifteen thousand inhabitants. It owes all of its importance to the Suez Canal. There were several steamers anchored off Suez, awaiting their turn to enter the canal. The steamers must move slowly, so as not to break down the sides of the canal, and they must keep a certain distance apart. At regular intervals, there are turn-outs, like the switches and side-tracks on a railway, where the vessels pass one another.

Many of the passengers took the train from Suez to Cairo. But Mr. Anson was afraid to prolong their stay in such an unhealthy climate as that of Egypt, and so kept with the steamer till it reached Port Said, at the end of the Suez Canal. Here he took a steamer, on which were hundreds of Moslem pilgrims returning from Mecca, and crossed the Mediterranean, passing by the island of Crete, and through the Grecian Archipelago, until the Hellespont, or Dardanelles—across which Leander, and, many centuries later, Lord Byron, swam—into the Sea of Marmora, and thence to Constantinople.

"It seems to me," said Mrs. Anson, as they approached Constantinople, "that I have never seen any lovelier view than this. It is so bright, so varied in outline, and so gorgeous in splendid buildings. Those strange old fortifications, the roofs, the domes, the minarets of Stamboul"—as the main part of Constantinople is named—"on the left, and the cemeteries and the cypress groves on the Asiatic shores, the Bosphorus opening, and the scenery beyond, present, indeed, a beautiful picture."

"But wait a little," suggested one of their fellow-passengers, an English resident of Constantinople, "and a grander view than even this will be before you. There; now we shall go around the Seraglio Point into the Golden Horn. See, to the south, here, the seven low hills, crowned with their domes and slender minarets and odd-looking houses. Then, over on the north, in Galata, with its crowded buildings, and on the heights of Pera the splendid residences of the European embassies. Behind us, now, we have left Scutari."

"It is, indeed, a specimen of Oriental splendor," said Mr. Anson.

By the advice of their English acquaintance, they took rooms in the Hotel d'Angleterre, in Pera, to which they were taken by the agent of the hotel, who looked after their landing.

Under the guidance of a "dragoman," or guide, the Ansons went to visit the Sultan's Seraglio, several of the mosques, and even across to Scutari, to see the Whirling Dervishes. On several of these occasions Mrs. Anson was compelled to remain in her room at the hotel; the fever seemed to have taken a fresh hold upon her. Mr. Anson was in some alarm about her, and it interfered not a little with his enjoyment. To the children, it seemed as if their mother was but weary; and the bright colors, the quaint buildings, the odd costumes, were a source of unvarying delight.

Taking a carriage one morning, they crossed the New Harbor Bridge, and driving around by the railway depot, they passed the Seraglio, and

MOSQUE OF ST. SOPHIA.

stopped before the Mosque of St. Sophia, just adjoining.

"The Sultan's women have not far to go to church," suggested Bertie.

"Do you know why Constantinople is so called, Bertie?" asked Mr. Anson.

"Yes, sir; after Constantine the Great. He founded the city, did he not?"

"Oh, no," replied his father. "You will have to brush up your history. It was founded nearly a thousand years before, and was called Byzantium. Constantine simply adopted the ruined Byzantium as his capital, and raised it to a yet greater glory. Did you ever hear the story of the founding of Byzantium?"

"No, sir."

"I will tell it to you. Nearly seven hundred years before Jesus was born, some Megarian emigrants asked their oracle to tell them where to found a new city. 'Found your city opposite the land of the blind men,' was the advice. They traveled to find the 'land of the blind men.' When they came to Chalcedon—called Kadi Keui now—they at once perceived that the curving shores of the Golden Horn offered a site for a city far surpassing any place they had yet seen. Then they understood that the 'blind men' were they who could not see the advantages of the opposite shore. There they settled. St. Sophia—Sophia is the Greek word for wisdom, and refers to Jesus as the incarnation of wisdom—was, at the first, a Christian church. Its foundations were laid in the days of Constantine. It was destroyed several times, but was rebuilt with yet greater splendor. The emperor designed to surpass Solomon's Temple. The East was ransacked for beautiful marbles. Gold was used lavishly. The emperor said that an angel had revealed its plan in a dream. Now let us see it."

The Ansons first removed their shoes and put on slippers, as all are required to do in entering Moslem mosques; then they went to the gallery from which they could have a view of the magnificent interior.

"The great dome seems to hang in the air," said Bessie. "These beautiful columns come, so I have read, from many old temples in Egypt, Ephesus, and Athens. The building was sixteen years in erecting. When it was finished, the emperor ran in, exclaiming: 'God be praised, who hath esteemed me worthy to complete such a work. Solomon, I have surpassed thee!'"

Nearly an hour they tarried in the mosque, going from point to point; now they stood before the Mihrab, where the holy book, the Koran, is kept; now they approached the altar, or walked around under the great dome, whose circumference was less than the space between the columns, and which truly seemed to hang in the air, without visible supports. Whenever any Mohammedan came in to pray, he turned his face toward the Mihrab, and so to the southeast; the building being exactly square, and built in an exact line with the points of the compass, the worshipers thus oddly faced the corners of the mosque, and not the centre of the eastern side, where formerly stood the altar.

When they stood without, Bertie called attention to the crescent over the dome.

"That crescent is worth, so they say, fifty

thousand dollars in gold," remarked Mr. Anson.

"What does the crescent mean?" asked Bertie.

"About four hundred years before, the Macedonians had besieged the city of Byzantium. One dark night they intended to take the city by surprise. Just as they had commenced their assault, the clouds parted, and by the light of the crescent moon, the soldiers on the walls saw the enemy approaching. Thenceforth it became their symbol. When the Turks conquered Constantinople, they adopted it as their symbol."

Dismissing the carriage, they descended to the water's edge, and crossed in a small boat to Scutari, to the Ronfai Convent, where the Whirling Dervishes reside. It was just a little before one o'clock when they had arrived. The Dervishes entered and seated themselves in a circle, and prayed a short prayer five times over. Then rising, they began, at first slowly then more rapidly, to say, "*La ilah illallah,*"

THE WHIRLING DERVISHES.

meaning, "there is no God but God." They pronounced it thus: "*La-i-lah-il-la-lah.*" At the first syllable they bowed forward, at the second stood straight, at the third bent backward, and so on. Rapidly and yet more rapidly they seesawed up and down. Then the sheik, or leader, began to stamp. At once they seemed to increase their motion four-fold, and began to whirl round and round, and bend up and down like crazy men. All this time they cried out their sentence, which now sounded like one "*lah*," interrupted occasionally by "*hoo! yah hoo!*" meaning, "He, He is God." By-and-by they joined hands and swung to and fro, with their long hair flying like a cloud. Finally, some fell down foaming at the mouth, others swooned and were carried out. It became more than the Ansons could stand; Bertie's head seemed to be dizzy.

When they reached the hotel, Mr. Anson was met at the door by a servant, who told him that Mrs. Anson had been so ill that they had had to call in the doctor. He hastened to his room and found the doctor there.

CHAPTER XVII.

THE INVALID'S JOURNEY HOME.

"I AM Dr. Stevenson; this is Mr. Anson, I judge," spoke up the physician, quickly. "We have a rather sick lady here. Please tell me about her. I have but this moment reached here."

"It was when we were in Siam that my attention was first drawn to the fact that my wife was ill. I had thought, before that, that it was simply weariness."

"Where did you come from, before reaching Siam?" asked the doctor.

"From Canton, China, where we lived for quite a little while on the banks of the river."

"H'm, h'm, just so. The fever plainly. It is a hard thing for us Englishmen or Americans to stand the malarious atmosphere of such spots. I often wonder how the missionaries manage to live there for years. But, to get to business, you had better get this lady away from here as soon as possible. You can go to Switzerland, or you can go right to America. It will not require much more of an effort to cross the ocean, if she is a fair sailor."

"She has generally been better on the water than ashore," said Mr. Anson.

"So much the better. Get some thick clothing ready, because you will be going to much colder latitudes. In the meanwhile, I will leave some medicine to act as a tonic for your wife. We cannot reach the cause of the trouble with medicine; that you will have to leave to the sea voyage to accomplish. How are you going home? Have you fixed on a plan?"

"I had thought to take the Austrian Lloyd's mail steamer to Trieste, and thence by Venice, Milan, Turin, and across the Alps into France, and thence to England," replied Mr. Anson.

"Have you bought tickets for that route?"

"No, for I have made no fixed plan yet."

"You are wise not to have done so, for one never knows what may happen. I would suggest that you take one of Burns and McIver's first-class Liverpool steamers, and go all the way to America by water. You can stop at Malta and Gibraltar. You can lie over in England as long as you please. However, there is no place like home; and, unless your wife gets thoroughly well, you had better go right on to the States."

"Thank you, doctor; I will study the matter over. It is almost certain that I will do as you suggest."

In a week Mrs. Anson was able to leave her bed, and they were soon sailing away from Asia to the home-land westward. The voyage through the Mediterranean was especially enjoyable, for the air was balmy and mild, and the sea smooth. Daily, Mrs. Anson was carried on deck, and carefully screened from the sun's rays and from draughts of air. She thus mended rapidly. The rest of the family hung about the convalescent, now reading to her, now chatting with her, now singing in concert, now discussing the journey over which they had come, or forecasting their arrival at home. They never wearied when talking over the various interesting things they had seen from the day when they first started for their long tour. Of course they found that the hours flew apace.

At Malta, Bertie and his father paid a flying visit to St. John's Cathedral, with the Crusaders' graves. They climbed the fortress towers, to obtain the beautiful view over the harbors. Four days later, Gibraltar was reached. The six hours' stay of the steamer was utilized by Mr. Anson and Bertie to visit the castle and the formidable batteries. The time was too short to allow them to climb the heights of the Rock of Gibraltar, towering upward to a height of twelve hundred feet.

The glassy green ocean now appeared, changing from the deep blue of the sea. Without any delay, the Ansons reached Liverpool with but time to be transferred to the Cunarder about to start for New York. Unvarying kindness was shown on both the steamers to the invalid lady. A very pleasant friendship had sprung up between the passengers and officers, on the longer voyage from Constantinople to Liverpool. It was with genuine regret that they parted company at Liverpool.

A few days after leaving Queenstown, Ireland, Mrs. Anson was lying upon her easy sea-chair, knitting. Bertie sat by her side, reading his Bible.

"What are you reading, my son? Read it to me, will you not?"

"I was reading the seventeenth chapter of John's Gospel, and I stopped reading and began thinking over this verse: 'As thou hast sent me into the world, even so have I sent them into the world.'"

"What did you think of it?" asked his mother.

"Why, that Jesus was a foreign missionary.

Then I thought that his disciples were to be like him, and to go into the world too. But, mamma, all Christians can't go."

"No, my son; some only can go, and some must send them. Your papa could not go; I suppose"—with a smile—"that I should get too sick, if I were to go, even if your papa was not my husband."

"Well, mamma, how can anybody know certainly just whether he ought to go, or to stay?"

"Let us be frank with each other, Bertie. Are you thinking of yourself?"

"Why, yes, mamma, I believe I am."

"You are a Christian, yourself, my son. That is the first thing. You cannot tell the gospel to others until you have experienced its power yourself. Then, too, you have tried—I have seen it when you thought I did not notice it—to persuade some of your school friends to be Christians."

"Why, of course, mamma; I could not help that," interrupted Bertie.

"That is just it; you did it so naturally that it shows that you have the missionary spirit. Now, the next thing is, where are you most needed, and for what work are you most fitted? These are two most important questions. I do not know that you are old enough to answer the last question. One moment, papa"—calling to Mr. Anson, who was leisurely pacing the deck—"can you help us?" And she detailed the conversation thus far.

"Why," said he, "Bertie's character has so far shown itself that I think we can determine if he has, even undeveloped as yet, the germs of those qualities needed for missionary work at home and abroad. He has a sound body for a foundation."

"Yes," added his wife, "we have taken pains with that from babyhood."

"Then, too," continued Mr. Anson, "he seemed to pick up quite easily the German, as it is spoken in the German quarter of our town. He gets along fairly well at school. I do not know that he lacks any of the qualifications needed by a foreign missionary, except such as may be given him in the course of his education."

"Well, we can let that stand. How about the need for missionaries?" asked Mrs. Anson.

"Well, there are needy fields in the territories and in the large cities in the Eastern States," said Mr. Anson.

"But," said Bertie, "there are none as needy as the countries of Asia, and the great cities other than the ones where the steamers stop. It seems to me, papa, that the people are so low, so superstitious, so wicked, that they ought to have more missionaries to preach to them about Jesus. I can't call to mind the beautiful temples we have seen without thinking of the way they worship in them, and the idols to whom they pray. I think of it most of the time."

"Perhaps God is leading you towards giving yourself to be a missionary. You must ask him about it."

"I have, papa; and I will keep on asking."

"I believe," added Mrs. Anson, "that the noble example of the godly men whom we met on our tour, and their earnest work, has made *me* feel an intense interest in their work, and that it has impressed Bertie also."

"I do not doubt it," said Mr. Anson.

Just then the gong sounding for luncheon interrupted the conversation.

That same evening, chancing to be alone, the parents began to talk of the morning's conversation.

"I do not question that our Heavenly Father is leading Bertie to be willing to give himself to Christ's service in heathen lands, and that it will come about that, unless something should interpose, we shall see our boy a foreign missionary," Mrs. Anson said.

"God grant it! even if it be hard for us to send him far from us," answered Mr. Anson.

"But I have been thinking of Bessie. She, too, seems impressed by what she has seen, and those whom she has met. Yet she has said nothing about becoming a missionary."

"Well, my dear wife, we do not know what has been passing in her mind. Neither do we know but that God will let the seeds sown in this journey lie in her heart until some later occurrence may develop them. In the meanwhile, I am sure that our little Mission Band will be the better by having had its representatives in foreign lands."

We need not follow the Ansons to their home in Illinois. They were welcomed with joy by the people of their congregation, both old and young. For awhile, there seemed danger lest Mr. Anson should be overtaxed by the demands upon him from other churches to come and tell of his travels. Finally, however, he reduced it to system; and many were the times that he thanked God for the privilege he had enjoyed of seeing for himself the mission work of Asia, and for the further privilege of telling others what he had seen and learned on his long tour.

He soon saw the results, in an increased interest in the great work among the members of the churches that he visited.

It was nearly a year before Mrs. Anson's health was fully restored. Her experience in this direction enabled both her husband and herself to sympathize more fully than they could otherwise have done with invalided missionaries.

THE END.

www.ingramcontent.com/pod-product-compliance
Lightning Source LLC
Chambersburg PA
CBHW032054230426
43672CB00009B/1586